THE AFTERSHOCK

of Neoliberal Education:

Notes from "The Sub"

An exposé of public schools in
San Francisco & Marin County, California

By Barbara McVeigh
Unedited and Raw

The Aftershock of Neoliberal Education: Notes from "The Sub"

Copyright © 2021 by Barbara McVeigh. All rights reserved.

The right of Barbara McVeigh to be identified as the author of this work has been asserted by him in accordance with the Copyright, Design and Patents act 1988.

No part of this book may be reproduced, copied or used in any form or manner whatsoever without written permission, except in the case of brief quotations in reviews and critical articles.

Cover Design & Interior design by Velin@Perseus-Design.com

Paperback ISBN: 978-0-9989111-5-1

"If you feel that your catalyst may be a boat, that your instinct leads you to the sea, (that water-land-life left long ago), then clothe yourself in a vessel of wood, a work of art, that you, YOU can create, restore and preserve . . . Ah you loving men! You destroy the creatures of field and forest, and mine the noble metal to satisfy your purpose; your fleeting, vague, ambient, self destructive purpose. To destroy yesterday and not preserve today is a crime against tomorrow. Some poor souls call that progress."

- **Excerpt from *Flotsom and Jetsam*, Donald Keleher.**

The early childhood education centers in Reggio Emilia were established in response to the fascist experience in post WWII, which had "taught them that people who conformed and obeyed were dangerous...in building a new society it was imperative to safeguard and communicate that lesson and nurture and maintain a vision of children who can think and act for themselves."

- **Loris Malaguzzi Founder of Reggio Emilio**

Contents

Introduction	1
2018	12
2021 - Full Circle	186
Afterwards	189

Introduction

For over one year I served as a substitute teacher in San Francisco and Marin County public schools in California. In that effort, I had opportunity to observe and learn about our current state of public education. Frankly, I often witnessed nothing less than daily trauma, abuse and often times a disregard for what should be natural - a respect toward another human being. My notes herein are not meant to shame or blame, they are to expose a toxic system of disrespect and inadequate schooling so we can reconcile the challenges we have as a means to heal and reshape who and what we are as California and as an American society.

Our schools are a mess and given we are in extreme challenges with climate change, working poor, billionaire corruption and collapse of our American civil liberties, we can acknowledge our public schools have failed us. We have overworked teachers, underpaid educators, crowded schools, bully kids running classrooms, bad food, trash, abusive teaching practices and misinformed pedagogical approaches that got rolled out by corrupt billionaires, as our classrooms serve as commericialized platforms for big tech and junk media.

Education can become the next great frontier to broaden the context of what it means to nurture and cultivate well balanced, happy children who can thrive in and solve a growing environmental crisis that has been exacerbated under the neoliberal decades these last forty years, post President Jimmy Carter who tried to set it right, a four decade span which should be labeled "The Reagan Era".

Why do I call these last 40 years The Reagan Era? For some strange reason, beyond my explanation, we have, as a society, not been able to make the connections of what President Ronald Reagan's neoliberal policies have done to the spirit of our nation, all of which can be reflected in our public educational institutions. The aftermath of Reaganomics, knock down of unions and Fairness Doctrine Ruling and more have led to consequences akin to "the hell we live with today," as written by journalist Maximilian Alvarez of The Real News. Reagan's policies gave the keys to corrupt billionaires to dominate and control a democracy, an economic trickle that has turned into a cascade of medical, corporate, educational and tech tyranny. This conversation is not limited to the

The Aftershock of Neoliberal Education

Republican Party narrative. The essence of Reagan's corrupt policies have been abused hypocritically by the Democratic Party, namely and specifically by Congresswoman Nancy Pelosi, US Senator Diane Feinstein and California Governor Gavin Newsom. As a substitute teacher, I was in the thick of this hypocrisy in both counties who label themselves Liberal Democrats.

For example, Starr King, a coveted abolitionist and highly respected by President Abraham Lincoln, is buried in San Francisco. His statue stood for over seven decades in Washington DC, as a symbol of the spirit of California. Starr King was credited for keeping the union together during The Civil War. A mountain in Yosemite is named after him and a spiritual school in Berkeley carries his name. Most people have no idea who he is, an example of how our neoliberal education gave rise to criminals while deleting the true heroes and other great leaders from the textbooks. In 2013 Congresswoman Pelosi removed King's statue and replaced it with a statue of Republican President Ronald Reagan, with no opportunity for public comment. Reagan today stands next to Missionary Junipera Serra, whom many credit with genocide of Native Americans. California Governor Newsom sanctioned a Ronald Reagan Day, February 6. Reagan carries the soul of neoliberalism in our nation, starting with our schooling.

Let me repeat that. Junipera Serra and Ronald Reagan serve as California's inspirational spirit as statues in Washington, DC. How did that get past us? Not a woman, not a California Indigenous leader, and not a regular citizen. We have a religious figure and a corrupt politician representing us and put there by a political leader who banked politically on this action.

Treason is defined as the betrayal of someone's trust or confidence. I raise my hand boldly, as I learned to do with an education in school. These acts of political hypocrisy by Newsom, Pelosi and Feinstein who have built a career pointing the fingers at Republicans as the enemy while heralding a Republican president who has ruined not only this state of California but the entire planet with climate change should be tried with treason, full stop.

As a KQED public radio intern years ago, I used to interview Nancy Pelosi during the early years of her political career I had great admiration for her. Just a few years after completing my memoir *Redemption, How Ronald Reagan Nearly Ruined My Life*, I had a chance to meet her at a local town hall meeting in Marin County. I was so happy to give her a copy of my book believing she would value it. I mean, here is a citizen stepping up to describe how Reagan's policies, The GOP "Hero" undermined so many of our economic, political and environmental issues. Instead of thanking me, Pelosi turned as white as a ghost and said "Oh, my god." She didn't even look up at me and she scurried away into the crowd. I was left with such curiosity why she reacted in such a way. It took me weeks to understand, after researching on line, that Nancy Pelosi held Nancy Reagan's hand while raising the Reagan statue in Washington DC. Why would a Democrat herald a Republican President? This curiosity led me to other democrats who have upheld Reagan, including President Barack and Michelle Obama.

Find the humor. There is a lot of comedy filling these following pages. You have to laugh at the absurdity of being human so we can become humbled, recognizing our blind spots in our effort to excel. During my time at the public schools, I saw the good intentions by many teachers, administrators and parents, good people in a bad system that continues to contort onto itself with every new twist and turn. Perhaps we can look at education entirely differently after you read what I experienced, as a substitute teacher, a sneak peak into the inner workings of our classrooms from elite Marin County to the underfunded inner city schools of San Francisco struggling while big tech looms, junk food corporations prey on our children and nature is being forgotten. We can learn. Let's break out of the classroom and choose to be bold and courageous, like our great writers, leaders and thinkers have always encouraged us to be. Let's believe our history lessons were valuable. And let's be the creators of a new age. We have the tools and the inspiration everywhere around us.

On a personal and professional level, as a substitute teacher, I was daily abused while literally making less per hour than a high school babysitter while helping to maintain a public school image that drives nearby property values, state grants and the future of our children. What kept me going? I thought of all those before me who did this work and never received credit. I thought of all the other teachers and subs who get constantly abused. This testimony is in their honor.

I'm a filmmaker and photographer. I've traveled around the world listening to stories of the people, not the politicians, including citizens of Albania, India, Cuba, China, Europe and Eastern Europe. I have something to offer instead of just reading a page from a boring book and sticking a silly animated digital cartoon in the faces of children for an hour! I could be construed as an opportunity rather than a mere warm body filling a void. I hear it said all the time about substitute teachers: "You just need a college degree and a CBEST test..." a quote directly from Jeffery M. Freitas, President of the school union while advocating for Newsom's election during the 2021 recall. Talk about condescending! It's been the game in our public system.

What's also a defining argument as we challenge our public schools is why it has become a non discussion that those with money can choose any school for their child. Shouldn't that be considered an unjust system? There are other educational paradigms that have existed far longer and have survived the test of time other than Gate's recent Common Core experiments and heavy technology intrusions. One of those is the 100 year old Waldorf pedagogy, one that could highly serve a population that is sickened by the commercialization/media saturation in our schools. Waldorf education strives to educate the whole child, with a robust curriculum including deep arts, nature, civility, healthy eating, gratitude, respect and more, aspects of what make us human.

Let's shake up the system because when kids see the adults actually value our educational system, the kids will start to respect it too. Kids could get a good dose of real life, good stories and be thrilled about coming to school instead of counting the days until they get released from behind the chainlink fences, tech zombie screens and junk food cafeteria food. End *"Substitism!"* No more dumping and hating the substitute teacher who gets paid shit wages, endures daily abuse! Perhaps we'll find world peace, democracy and an enlightened generation!

Don't laugh. It could happen.

Enjoy.

First Day of Kindergarten, Marin County, CA 2021

School has been out for months. They have called it a pandemic. Some could extend that to a big tech and big pharma coup, given that 5G and Elon Musk's Starlink also launched the first week of the lockdowns while no one was watching and government stimulus bills padded big tech and big pharma with billions, making new billions for billionaires while regular folks went belly up, but whatever. Right now I'm just observing the aftermath and trying to recoup financially before I'm out on the streets.

I place a number of masked overweight, obese kids in line to sit six feet apart, on the cold asphalt. It's 8am Wednesday morning, the first day of Kindergarten. Parents are behind the chainlink fence with their cameras. Some kids are crying and are being ignored as teachers grab the little ones who have no idea where they need to go. I see a young black mother behind the chain linked fence seeking her child in the line up of kids. I scan the crowd and racially profile a child - yes, it was the only way. I see her. One black child in a sea of Latino kids. I squat next to the sweet child all dressed up with ribbons and colorful clips in her hair. A new dress and white socks up to her knees. I tell the child to look up and point to her mother who snaps a photo from afar. It's a picture to celebrate the child's first day of school, one that will be in their photo album for years to come, a reminder of the insanity of her first day of kindergarten. Her mother smiles at me and thanks me, though I simply want to apologize to her. I see she's worried. I am too, but I can't tell her that. I want to tell the mother how sorry I am her sweet kindergarten child has to endure the mania adults have created. And this day is NOT how the first day of school should ever be for new students, children three to five years out of the womb.

Kids are eating breakfast as they sit on the cold concrete ground. A combination of plastic wrapped sliced apples, plastic wrapped sugary pastry, a plastic tub of sugary yogurt. Milk. Plastic wrapped cheese stick. Some kids can't do criss cross applesauce due to their obesity. Apparently obesity has risen this past year during lockdowns and more, a warning the Surgeon General had called out in 2001, that obesity is an epidemic and a pandemic in the making. Nothing has been done and today our country faces the fact that one out of eight children are obese. Some have called this a national security threat when young people are being turned down from military service.

I watch in horror, but keep a smile on under my own mask as I try to breathe.

I join a classroom. A white obese teacher brings out a book to read to the children. It's about families and how the classroom is going to be a "family". I cringe. Why do I cringe? I do so because the story of Canadian indigenous children found buried in a school has reached international news. I look at the children in the classroom, many of whom are from Guatemala and likely many are Mayan indigenous. The teacher continues to read how they will spend almost more waking hours together than they do with their own families. She reads about brothers and sisters fighting at home but at school won't have to worry about that problem.

I shudder. I recall my own education about the Mayan indigenous people. I didn't even know massive Mayan temples existed just south of the border until I graduated from high school, put on a back pack and headed to Mexico and Guatemala with the intention to uproot every lie I was indoctrinated with.

I see the Kindergarten teacher clearly lacks the respect for the Latin family ethos and does not understand her audience. The Latin community, with specific focus on Central Americans, are deeply committed to families, brothers, sisters, aunties and more. And her book does nothing but deprive them of that respect while trying to validate her idea that the classroom is a family.

"Know your place," I want to say to the teacher. But, I don't. Not yet.

The Aftershock of Neoliberal Education

I'm traumatized watching children in their masks, filled with wet bacteria. Some already have a patch of moisture by the nose. When they talk, their voice is muffled. No smiles. Just eyes darting around, looking down or tears being shed.

"Get into your square, Jose! Criss cross applesauce." The teacher says to a child. He isn't sitting perfectly centered in his square on the carpet. Another child sits alone crying.

I am witnessing madness, indoctrination, lack of ability to understand a child, rhythm and respect. This is what we are teaching our children in public schools. And as a new year begins, I reflect on the nothing less than trauma I had experienced in 1981 and the last 40 years, an era , that has put millions into poverty, brought on climate change full tilt and traumatized a generation of children.

- 2018 -

Private School, Marin County, June 2018

I had stepped into a second and third grade mixed classroom to take over for a popular teacher. He had paternal leave when his baby was born and it was quite sudden. To make matters more complicated, the private school was closing after nearly 30 years due to financial challenges. I walked into the classroom with no budget, no deep understanding where each of the kids stood academically, emotionally or socially and there were two months left of school. One child sat at her desk with piles of books acting as a barrier between her and her teacher, keeping her head low. Another child who was fairly new could not sit still for more than five minutes without outbursts, literally running like the Tasmanian Devil around the classroom. Several of the children came with parents who clearly let me know that they knew more than I did and challenged me on many decisions I made, including where to place the children when they sat in morning circle. This was going to be a tough job. But, I'm tough.

"Make sure my son sits next to a quiet girl," one parent told me. She wanted the quiet girl to manage her son. Of course, she gave no thought to the girl who would disrupted by her son constantly. It was a direct attack, one that I would witness often. Position boys favorably and who cares about the girls. That was my thought.

The three months became nothing less than a symbolic insane asylum. At the end of it all, you would have seen my ratted hair, bags under my eyes and exhaustion. It was by the far the toughest job I ever loved, one that nearly kicked my ass. What happened and what went right?

I did my best in those months dedicating every waking hour I had to their curriculum, field trips and projects. It opened my eyes to the way many parents treat teachers, those dedicated to their children. It seemed at times I was working for the parents, not the children. I witnessed amazing teachers and staff and I felt bad that more respect was not delivered to them, as I learned teaching is not about clocking in and out. It takes your soul and your heart and those things cannot be measured by statistical numbers.

I can say the girl cleaned up her desk of the wall of books and hugged me. That alone gave me an A on my effort and rebooted my soul and heart.

I'd get my paycheck at the end of week and wonder how I'd pay rent for the month, as I slept on a sofa and rented out my bedroom in a two bedroom in Marin County, as a single mother recently divorced and trying to get my life back on track.

Amazingly, just twenty-five years ago I could work a 30 hour job at $13/hour and live in a small apartment in San Francisco AND get myself through college DEBT FREE. I'd have enough money for an airline ticket to teach at a university in China and savings to get me through the year. That is an impossible feat today. It's nearly impossible for a TEACHER to even afford rent in a shared small apartment. As a substitute teacher needing credentials, four year university degree, CBEST exams and updated expensive annual credentials, participate in unpaid training hours and meetings while dealing with young people who have major social and emotional needs, are violent, depressed and sometimes need their butts wiped, my hourly pay is about $17.50 an hour. I go to a food bank to make ends meet AND still pay off a $18,000 loan for my Master's Degree, that helped pay for manicured gardens at my former graduate school. Our whole system is screwed up.

And somehow I still love the work and refuse to quit as a substitute teacher.

September 2019, Marin County

Worksheets. Some complain there are too many. Perhaps a legit complaint and I could possibly agree. But today's worksheet, a math game, seems rather benign and not too bad. Kids partner up and there's

The Aftershock of Neoliberal Education

chatter, again benign for a 3rd grade class. I'm the sub for the day and I walk the aisles talking to the kids as they play their dice game, doodle, cheer or gossip when they think I'm not paying attention. It all seemed to be going okay until I watched a team of adults walk in to observe me. "What did I do wrong?" I wanted to ask initially. Are they suspicious of me? It's a thought that passes quickly when one of the adults approaches me.

"We are going to try out a math teacher. Are you okay with that?"

Of course I was okay with that. I suck at math and even have to question my third grade level, I think to myself with humor.

In walks an older teacher. She asks all the children to come to the front rug but struggles to get the kids into a circle. Her instructions were unclear and she kept blaming the kids for not listening. Then she told the kids how great of a math teacher she is and the tools she's using are the most progressive today. She had just returned from South America teaching village children there, as if the exotic travel to a Spanish speaking country validates her greatness. That's how it came off.

I watched. Heck, maybe I could learn something. My eagerness, though, quickly turned to doom and gloom. She was plugging in her computer, pulling down the white screen and then proceeded to tell the kids that they no longer have to play math games against each other. Now, they can do that with the computer!

I know my jaw must have dropped.

She proceeded to go over the rules of the game, I watched the computer graphics dazzle and flash. The kids fell silent. One by one the teacher called on the kids to ask for right answers or to play the game with the computer. After the teacher circulated around the room with the other adults, pointing out needless doodling and wasted paper. She had them hooked and dazzled. I looked at the kids and wanted to apologize. There would be no more chatter during math games. Instead, zoned eyeballs would widen staring at screens in silence.

She walked the aisles looking at the math worksheets and games the kids had been doing before she had walked in. Many were decorated with doodles of fanciful loops, Pac Man images and daisies.

"See, they can't waste time doodling with this math system," she said.

Another teacher with her nodded, as if her words were gold. She was a teacher selling a product, a curriculum and machines that would make Bill Gates proud.

Me? I knew in my gut these changes were not good. Fool's gold it was. After all, it's not just math and number crunching children learn when they work together, and, yes, doodle. They are developing social skills, sharing laughter, making human connection. Most importantly? Learning how to work with another human being. We are becoming misguided in our effort to get the answers right by eliminating one of the most important elements in our society - human contact and civility.

My eyes remained wide open as I continued the substitute teaching journey, acknowledging that while we were doodling, the technology has overtaken our schools, reducing so much curriculum into a game unfit for humans, a charade that should end full stop.

September 2019, San Francisco

I have an early morning meeting with the county school district. I have to prove I have no criminal record. I must have done this countless times now, ensuring a good budget for Homeland Security. Another $60 plus into their revenue stream. You'd think if they were so secure they wouldn't make you do this every time you get a new job. They extract from teachers who make criminal wages while our government officials bank on the fees. You can be assured their monthly income is a fair wage.

I was almost made guilty for being late. The rush hour traffic into San Francisco was extreme this morning and with that anxiety and that of walking into an office to prove my innocence, I knew being late would not be the right impression for them. I needed work. I was innocent even if I felt like I was on my way to criminal levels of insanity at times with survival.

Being in San Francisco, though, always settles me. It's a place where I healed thirty years ago, where I went to college, hung out at cafes when the Beat Generation spirit was still alive, worked and grew into an adult during my 20s recovering still, emotionally and financially, from my family's 1981 National Strike against the neoliberal kingpin Ronald Reagan. It's where I met my husband/partner of twenty five years, even if he's an ex. It's where I gave birth to my son. It's where I found myself, Alan Ginsberg and dead bohemians speaking loud through books, poetry and songs. In those days, San Francisco had edge and grace.

But it's changed.

I arrive at the third floor and walk into an empty of human existence Human Resources office. There it was. I stood there in front of an empty desk with a phone sitting on it. There was no one within eyesight. I waited longer, checking my watch. A man walked passed me, uninterested in saying hello until I stopped him. I needed to talk to someone for my appointment.

He pointed to the phone, as if I were stupid. Yes, that phone on the desk. But I needed a number. An identity, in order to use it. I didn't have one. I was a nonhuman at this stage. After I proved my innocence, perhaps someone would talk to me or better yet, I'd get a number. I had forgotten to insert the chip into my arm to prove my identity. Just kidding, but that's what it felt like.

"It's asking for a number and I don't have a number," I say to a man who looks at me, walking assuredly toward me with a blank expression.

"You push the blue button."

Great! A clear indication that I am stupid! Of course, the blue button! How did a miss that! I may not prove to be a criminal, but I just demonstrated my stupidity. A blue button with no instructions!

Soon enough a young enough man, cool hip sort of dude, approaches me. It's all business. No chit chat.

"You have paperwork?" He spoke like a robot. "You must have this and that and that and this. . ."

It was chilling. No facial expression. No warmth. I try to break the ice. Me? As always, I try to break the ice and bring some warmth to the show.

"How long have you been here?" I ask.

He looks at me over his eye glasses "Four years"

"Oh, you must have seen a lot!" I say.

"I cannot comment on that question. I do my job. I do my job well. And I get paid. Now, to the waiting room and fill out these highlighted forms."

Sure enough, signing my life away that I am not a felon. I think carefully. Am I sure I'm not a felon? What if I have some PTSD brain block of something I did and I can't remember. I'll get into bigger trouble by signing that I have no criminal record? My mind begins to play tricks.

I turn in the documents. He takes me into the next room and puts on black gloves. Oh, no.

"You stand over on the black square and put your bag there," he says.

The Aftershock of Neoliberal Education

I do as I'm told.

"Yes, I am 100 feet from that spot," he says.

I look at him. "Excuse me?" I say but he doesn't reply to me. I continue to get ready thinking that maybe I made a mistake in hearing something from him.

"No, that's not right," he says.

I'm merely putting my bag down while standing on the black mat. What could I be doing wrong.? I look at him quizzically and then more carefully. Is he talking to himself? Maybe he's the crazy one.

"That's right," he says to the tooth in his ear. He wags his finger at me. He's having another conversation with the Star Trek Enterprise. And I feel relieved.

He calls me over to a small machine. "Put your thumb there," he says. He takes my hand, controlling my hand with each finger print being pressed to the machine. I can feel an anger in him. I can feel a lack of love. I try to imagine who he is inside as he presses my fingers to a machine that will go into a national system to find out if I'm a bad guy. There's no emotion. No warmth. He's a machine. I swear. He was a machine. And he scared me.

I wondered then who this young man really is. And what has happened to our collective humanness, laughter, chit chat and general decorum of being human beings.

"The people behind the screen will contact you in two or three days, that's all Mrs. McVeigh."

Behind the screen. Yes, one would wonder.

The City that I loved has changed. And I start to imagine what it will be like in the classrooms, unless I get locked up before then. But, maybe we all are locked up right now.

September, 2018 Marin County

One of the most privileged schools in Marin County. A City that even had the ability to tell Habitat for Humanity to get lost a few years back when the much beloved organization tried to build a few houses for a few needy people. Cappuccinos are $6, about half the hourly wage of the immigrant barista behind the counter. About a third of my hourly wage.

I once visited a friend at the tip, in Belvedere, one of the most elite hoods near Tiburon. I was driving an old Infiniti that had problems going in reverse. You had to give it extra gas. There I was on an incline to

The Aftershock of Neoliberal Education

reverse. I had mistakenly put my wallet on top of the car when I had gotten in. I reversed hard, making a loud screeching sound, then turned left and drove away. It was the next day or so I got a call from the Tiburon police. They had found my wallet! I hadn't even made the connection until then as to how I had lost the wallet.

I arrived at the station happily at first, pleased with the police but they didn't seem pleased with me. Very sternly they ordered me into the back room for some questioning. Questioning?

The report had been stated that a neighbor had spotted a car screeching and speeding away. After a bold turn before racing away someone threw a wallet out the window. Seriously! I almost started to laugh until I saw how stern the police were looking at me and scrutinizing my identification. My own explanation did not suit them. They wanted more. They wanted something. ANYTHING. There were no donut shops in Tiburon.

"Who was I visiting?" one asked me.

"A friend's house", I said, suddenly feeling guilty for no reason at all. They ran a check on my identification, another buck for Homeland Security? They asked me absurd questions. Where did I live? What do I do for a living?

"Dude, I'm on your team. I am a Marin County resident!" I wanted to scream.

That did not matter. They were bored and this was likely the most exciting case they had had in a long time. They were hoping. They were praying. I could see it in their eyes. They so wanted to arrest SOMEONE! Some action, please! I could hear it in their minds.

Finally, with enough talk, I walked out of that police station with an uncomfortable feeling that the police were not on my side.

So, back to the school, as I was saying. I was told I'd work with kids with special needs.

I had really no idea what that means, given the term these days is so loosely used. I'm believing we are all growing into individuals with special needs. What happens when that's just a given? Are we all still special?

I prepared myself to be present, cheery, positive and ready to do whatever I needed to do to support the kids.

And then I met them. Special kids? They were indeed. There were totally my kind of kids. They were artists who had not yet been identified as artists!

The Aftershock of Neoliberal Education

Sure. Some had a few challenges, but many had strong opinions and wit and hadn't lost their spirit yet. Some were shut down kids who were desperate. I could see that and more importantly, I could feel it.

Tech was being crammed down their throats. Stupid animated characters zipped across zombie screens telling stories of ancient Greece, making it into a shameful stupid cartoon episode. Or math equations were streaming up and down and sideways on their screens, enough to drive anyone insane and angry.

Then there was shaming, constant shaming. I don't even think the teacher knew how she was speaking to the kids, a form of gaslighting. Logins didn't work which pit the kids into anxiety, trying to do right and feeling they were doing wrong. I had seen that before. I even felt that at times myself!

I had this experience once before at my son's first grade class about ten years ago where I was asked to volunteer. The kids had each gotten their own IPAD, as if that gave the school kudos and upped their funding potential. Tech was moving its way into the classrooms, as early as first grade. I found it disgusting feeling there was literally no need for this kind of technology. It created anxiety and then zombie like addiction while the teacher sat back drinking their coffee watching the kids get "educated." This was a dangerous path. I knew it then and I'm screaming it today.

One girl blurted out suddenly, "I don't like school." She had been talking quietly to a girl next to her. The other teacher in the classroom heard her say these words. And he launched. "Do you have any idea how lucky you are to be in this school?" he admonished her. "You have everything, computers, everything!"

I stopped in that moment to witness an adult man shame a young coming of age girl who had an opinion. A pretty good opinion, for that matter too. But shaming her in front of the whole class while diminishing any opinion she might have?

I could see her grow small, as if ashamed and embarrassed in front of the whole class.

He then told her to go outside with him and I could imagine he was reading her the riot act. As she walked back in the classroom her face was so distraught. She was a young girl who was clearly having emotional challenges already and placed in a class deemed "special." She sat in her chair and stared ahead with a smile on her face that gave me chills. I remember that look and feeling, that idea that I'd do myself in one day and make them all feel bad about it, those people who pushed me down and made me hate myself. That was the look I saw on her face.

I had to leave the classroom, but I walked up straight to the face of that male teacher and told him, "Don't you EVER scream at a girl again." And went straight to the office and told the administrator, wondering if I'd ever get work there again. I was the newbie, after all. Would my complaining deem me a threat?

That young male teacher had had an opportunity to build a young girl up and validate her value that her ideas matter, whether he agreed with them or not. He could have teased out her feelings to find out WHY she hated school and then shown her ways to improve the conditions of the school that she doesn't like! That's teaching. That's empowering.

A man should NEVER be allowed to yell at a girl. Ever.

September 2018. Marin County

The lights are low. I stand in the back of the classroom while the teacher flicks on a video talk by someone heralding Elon Musk and his space age Mars ideas, a planet where we can find refuge after we kill our planet. It's pure Manifest Destiny on steroids. Tell me, where is the common sense of occupying a dead planet when we are sitting perfectly well on one that's alive? Right, a rocket will take us there, the power of a penis shaped instrument .. . the power. That's what it's all about. I swear to it.

No thank you, I think to myself during the class, unless we booster rockets on those bad boys and pack them full of the lying cheating politicians along with the billionaires. That's one solution.

My thoughts are lingering in my head only, as I listen and watch the teacher herald this billionaire, an exploiter of our democracy but somehow fits the bill today of being a hero. Not my hero. Today, for about $15 an hour, I am to help one particular table of four kids stay focused. "Stay on task," is the language that's popular. That means breathe down their necks and micromanage their actions. Maybe they are talkers or disruptors. I really don't know. Currently they are watching and listening to the video. So I watch and listen too.

After the talk about Elon Musk saving our lives, the teachers gives a task to these middle schoolers to come up with a plan to travel to Mars. What would their space craft look like? How much water should they bring? What are the essentials for surviving on Mars? He tells the kids to make a poster of their imaginary colonies on Mars and their spaceship to get there.

I held back my arm that was impulsively raising up high with a question. "Can we instead do this on planet Earth instead of extracting resources from Earth, a living planet, in order to populate a dead planet? But, my question would have tagged me as a trouble maker, disrupting this "dream," for the penis rocket to dominate the world. . . no, the galaxy. Yes, I'm crass. No, I'm not crass. Why would such a logical question NOT be part of this entire discussion? Why give power to the elites to solve our problems when we have the power, as the people, to live in harmony and respect with our natural world? I tighten my fist and take a deep breath. They call his project education. I call it manufactured propaganda.

The kids started drawing. I specifically admired art by a group of girls. Beautiful, pink shaped round rockets contained soft cushy seats instead of metallic, Star Trek robotic design. I sided with the girls. If I were shipping my ass to Mars, I better have a soft pretty cushion to sit on! How do you teach a hypothetical idea when even the teacher is not the pro? Is it called stupid teaching stupid? I'm a hard ass on this - let's stick to what we know and let them find their passions. I'm a hard ass. I need that soft cushion.

Meanwhile, I think about the ocean that we are acidifying rapidly, the source of 70% of our oxygen. We are killing ourselves shipping metallic objects into space with fuel that is killing our planet. . . to do WHAT exactly? Feel like Star Trek enterprise? This has got to stop. But, then I wonder if this is the Divine's humorous way of ensuring we virus like humans don't totally kill off the planet. We get fascinated with space instead of robbing our oceans of the last life on earth. Maybe there is a plan. Every time humans get involved with anything, they end up mucking it up. Right? I do wonder if we can prove ourselves wrong and actually begin to take responsibility for mucking up everything and reset our ways.

We are still alive, living on Earth. There is hope.

November 2021. Marin County

I could not bare watching the kindergarten class - set up like an overly organized corporate room with three adult women, two black and one white all shaming a little four year old white boy. He was just being a four year old little wiggly boy. But at the rate he's growing he will hate himself and everyone else around him for believing he is a bad boy because he let some paper drop to the floor.

I think back of my own kindergarten experience. A gentle and kind approach with games, nap schedules and lots of roly poly snakes made of clay, despite the teachers' attempts to have us make something more sophisticated. Hours smearing finger paint into streaks of eventual muddy colors and finding reason to play with Patty instead of Tommy on the playground.

The Aftershock of Neoliberal Education

I watch the scenario play out today and wonder how could this possibly become so ugly with a five year old boy.

These brutish women who resemble the horrid sisters in James and the Giant Peach shame a five year old little boy for making a mess. Shame, Marin County! Do I report this? Does this qualify as child abuse as a mandated reporter? Will I be charged with racism instead of calling out child abuse? These are teachers who have been in the classroom for over twenty years. They have clout. Me? a newbie comes in and reports them? Right, move over riots of Jessie Owens and George Floyd. I would create a maelstorm in this county for being bigotted, when honestly I'm being legal, as I'm a mandated reporter. I would lose my job in a heartbeat.

I overhear one of the black teachers say to one of the kids, "consider yourself lucky. You should have seen what I had to go through when I was a kid."

And there's the explanation. Trauma begets more trauma. The abused become the abusers. My heart aches for all of them. I simply wanted to hug her and apologize for all the hurt she had in her life.

But I couldn't. I needed to get out of the classroom to breathe air my own wellbeing first. Kindergarten should NOT be like this. And yet I just wanted to hug those kindergarten teachers with the most absolute love and say I am so sorry YOU had to endure abuse as a child. I am sorry what the world did to you. Maybe one day I can hug them. Maybe one day we'll understand another way of speaking to our children. I've read how the Inuit never show anger and are one of the happiest groups of people. They show getting angry is a form of not having control, and it's disrespected. Maybe we can all learn a different way and be inspired by them.

I go out to the playground and see the children like they should be and what is natural - chasing one another and breathing like me. Free, for a moment. I turn back and I see the mother of the little boy who got admonished for being too wiggly. He has scraps of paper under the table and the teachers are not letting him leave until he sweeps them up with an adult sized broom. The mother watches, being told her little boy is a bad boy. He has problems. She's a bad mother for having a bad son, is surely how she feels. She already looks tired and haggard, likely struggling to make ends meet. Maybe recently divorced. Who knows, but I see her exhaustion, her worry and no one is on her side. Because he is wiggly. The mother looks despondent.

My God, I think. Do I intervene? Right. And here my heart goes out to the teachers who are underpaid, come from trauma and likely receive little support putting trauma on the mother and the little boy. It's trauma everywhere. If I stop to intervene, I will be dismissed and likely not have a job again with the school. I'll be called racist or worse. And here I just want people to be happy and joyful and know how beautiful they are. The mother leaves with her little boy. Her little boy is crying. I watch feeling powerless.

November 2019. Marin County

I wonder, reading a book to teens about violent teens, does that invite more violence? I walked into a classroom with no instructions from the teacher. I've been down this road before. Okay, quick assessment, I think quick on my feet. I'm a professional substitute after all, and a thinking human being. What do they have on their desks? A book! I introduce myself - firm tone, look strong like a teacher who won't take bullshit, seeing there are definitely some boys who could challenge me. My firm voice knocks them down for the next few moments, as they assess me, try to figure me out, and I get through the roll sheet for the next three minutes without interruptions.

I get them reading for a few minutes quietly, silent reading. Actually they now call it SSR - what the hell does that mean? Right, Sustained Silent Reading. My god. Corporate acronym syndrome - CAS, has dominated our Normal Language Tendencies - NLT. It's called INSAN, another euphemism for "insanity" so we don't say the word and traumatize ourselves.

Stay firm, Barbara. It's a hard one for me, because I really just want to pull out the jokes and tell the kids "RUN FOR YOUR LIFE!"

The teacher's aid goes to the office for instructions. I know I can wing it, but. . . but . . . the instructions come in. Silent reading. Check for me. I got this. And hold a discussion about the book. No problem.

Well, heck the book *Outlanders* is all about rich kids and poor kids. So in our discussion we talk about empathy. One girl says the book is violent. Another girl says the amount of money has nothing to do with character. I'm liking these kids. Most of them are from the wealthiest part of this country. I think. Those with parents who benefitted from Reaganomics these past 40 years. Stop Barbara, don't go there. Dangerous talk in these parts. But why is it? They are reading a book about guns, anger, violence. Can't I tell my story about anger and violence? So I do. I tell them that I live in financial poverty, I sleep on a sofa and my father is a federal criminal, politically speaking, of course. Maybe' they've never seen a poor person before. I tell them what it's like to lose almost everything. What it's like to feel like the bad "guy." The anger that develops.

The Aftershock of Neoliberal Education

They stop dead with wide eyes. . . it's amazing how story telling can create lasting moments of Sustained Reality Listening Moments. (SRLM, *TM* by Barbara McVeigh)

Unclear of my instructions for the next class, I go to the office to double check the schedule. The verbal instructions I received are different than the written, so I want to confirm. I head to a class and walk in recognizing a teacher. She likes to make you feel stupid. Always.

"You don't know where you're going? She says to me right away.

She questions my questioning. That's a good gas lighting technique instead of just clarifying your question. But, I'm onto her.

"You need to do this and you don't remember it, do you?" she says to me, providing me my instructions for the class.

She's gaslighting me again! I know that language, but do the kids? Or do they just absorb it, blame themselves and questioning themselves? Create emotional trauma? I observe her and the kids who are hunched over at their desks. Yep, they've absorbed it. Well, I suppose that's good for the industry. . . ensures work for the school therapists.

This is a study class, a place to get homework help. It's a class for the kids who are falling behind or maybe have proved to be a challenge in some form or another. I'm ready for it. Many of them are doing math. Six grade math. Oh, no, I think to myself. I'm not even sure I can do six grade math anymore as I look at their books. It's gotten so complex. I position myself close to the kids reading books or have writing assignments, hoping and praying I'll be assigned to one of those students and utilize my writing skills instead.

My strategy didn't work. I'm told to sit down with a six grade student and help him with a math problem. "Uh, oh" I think, but I have to give it a try. I'm also instructed to not give the answer to the child but to help him work out troblem.

The student carried incredible anxiety as if these math problems and her challenge with them were seeding his own sense of failure and stupidity. After I looked at the math problems, my own anxiety grew, truth be told. A page filled with complicated symbols, minute instructions. What happened to simple instructions? We're all being converted into nerds! Social decorum, laughter, gone! Our beautiful souls beings stuck in a universe of figures, facts, shapes and graphs instead of big picture human meaning. Why? To be the next factory workers for Apple and Google? I try not to go there with such thinking but I naturally do.

The Aftershock of Neoliberal Education

I look carefully though. I'm going to crack this equation nut. I will be not leave this room feeling stupid. I see a written equation the student has written down, one that is critical for all the answers on the page.

I look carefully at the equation, uprooting all the years on my shoulders of feeling inadequate, stupid and wrong, digging deep into a core of math confidence. I start to question the equation and talk through it with the student. It doesn't make sense.

I can barely decipher the meaning of the graph and the equation the teacher gave him to work on. I continue my best not to curl into my "I'm stupid, stupid stupid!" rant I would have done in school myself years ago. "Come on Barbara, you can figure this out," I want to say out loud. I hurt my brain trying to understand the equation and what was being asked. But. . . but. . . I look at the equation and use my common sense approach. Why is the equation that and not this? I ask the student.

"That's what the teacher said it was," the student said, that same teacher who was an expert on gaslighting.

The more I look at the information she gave him, it just didn't add up. I kept questioning in my brain, coming from the point of view that I know nothing, humility. But then I become convinced. The gas lighting teacher made a mistake, so we had been trying to solve a problem based on the wrong equation the teacher had given the student! I fixed it. And with that fix, a whole host of other fixes fell like domino chips. "See, I can figure things out!" I wanted to scream to the student . . . though I think I wanted to scream that residual trauma to my own high school math teacher 40 years ago. I button my lip and move on. I see the hunched shoulders of the student relax just a bit and feel I did a small duty in the world.

Later in the day, I sit with two students in a class, one who is very heavy set screams with rage when she can't simply log in to a computer program.

"Excuse me, it's not a computer. It's an IPAD," a student quickly corrects me.

No, they all correct me. Good evidence that their substitute teacher is stupid and validates their own intelligence. That's the playing field I've entered and I'm happy to serve that, if the need is there! The upset student sees all the other kids who have successfully logged in. So she sits back and begins to sulk, hating herself, feeling stupid. She wants to draw, to free her mind. So she pulls out a pen and piece of paper and rebels. She doodles.

The one next to her is an empath. I see them immediately. They absorb all the energy around them.

The Aftershock of Neoliberal Education

They are truly gifts to society, the sensitive ones, who are abused the most because people can't understand them. She's clearly disturbed by the screaming and maintains herself, but you can see she's been traumatized. Closing her eyes, breathing calmly, as if she's been coached. She moves more slowly because she has been put with one of the "problem" children, she now defines herself that way. I want to raise my hand and shout - "you kids are the creative ones, the ones with unique personalities that cannot fit into a shape they want to cram you into!" These were the kids I wanted to hang out with. The artists!

My god, what are we doing to these children? School has become a zone for abuse, power and control instead of creativity, nurturing and rhythm.

My heart aches.

Education has become the practice of the football coach. Hyper talk instead of being real. Doing what you're told over and over again. Inflating egos for every minor thing. . . the kids see through this, at least some do. Others get dumbed down, lost. The teachers are doing their best to hold their jobs in this fragile landscape, and I feel at a loss of what to do except to write it all down. It's all I can do, for now.

September 2019, Marin County.

A twelve year old on a computer would not get off. Like an addict. I had to sit with him during class.

He had a syringe, not a needle type, one for water or something like that. His male teacher wigged out, as if it's proof in the pudding that he will be a drug addict, a loser in his adult life. He doesn't know how to handle him. The boy actually told me he wants to be an FBI agent one say. I liked this kid. But he needs support. He does not need a teacher who already believes he's a criminal.

I've seen that attitude before. We must believe in the best of our children. They are on a journey and we must support their journey.

October 2019, San Francisco

Seven kids. Great kids. Two assistants for seven kids. One assistant had been teaching for twenty seven years. I like her. A lot. I can see she sees the problems. High anxiety in kids. Low pay for teachers. She gave me high marks. She told me.

Parents make kids sign behavior contracts. Are we breeding lawyers? What nonsense is this? Another source of anxiety? Kids are 8 years old out of the womb. They are still learning how to sit at a table and eat food. There are no role models for this. Teachers walk around eating. We are NOT showing our kids how to be civilized yet we keep demanding them to be this high standard idea we have set for them. An illusion? Work needs to be rushed. Transition is from one mental exercise to the next. Rush rush rush rush. But of all classes so far, this class has been the best. One intense boy just wants to play war, make war machines. The violence our children have been conditioned to accept as normal is crazy. What the hell is a contract anyway? Yet another piece of societal mania that helps the lawyers in our society exploit those who are learning about our world? We're grooming out kids to let the lawyers exploit us instead of just learning how to have an intrinsic capacity at being civilized and kind.

I look at an assessment document, from therapists sitting on the teacher's desk:

Poor sense of rhythm or appears clumsy
Unable to gallop or skip
Does not initiate or participate in games
Fatigue or becomes tired easily.

Makes you see how therapists work at getting their clients - they are creating their clients!

And it goes on.

Check as applies: Frequently, Occasionally, Seldom:

Student is irritated by:
Standing in line
Unexpected touch
Does not like to wash hands
Avoids Crowded Places
Fearful when climbing equipment
Moves too slowly or too quickly
Unable to manage belongings or class materials
Difficulty in changing routines.

I can't believe my eyes that there are such assessments for 5 year olds!

People don't read anymore. That's a fact we have concluded in our society. And now I can understand why. Books and ideas are shoved down throats in classrooms with propaganda about being a good reader? Let the kids come to it themselves, at their own pace.

October 2019. San Francisco

I walk the streets of Noe and Castro, 16th Avenue, my old neighborhood of San Francisco. Trash scatters the sidewalks, limp figures cloaked in dirty blankets lay strewn like garbage or sit in corners as the sun begins to rise. What has happened to this beautiful city? This area used to be one of the most polished neighborhoods of San Francisco.

I can't find parking except for a two hour slot on the streets. Meter maids are already on the hunt. I saw one around the corner, those who are paid a salary to hunt those people like me. . . on the edge of financial security, knowing that I'll be squeezing each minute on the meter so I don't have to pay that extra dollar.

"I'm a substitute teacher," I want to scream. "I'm here to take care of your children, their teacher and your neighborhood school!" You'd think the city would be handing me a free hall pass or parking pass, on this one. Even the meter maid should be on my side. But, I saw that stick they poke out of their little cart, the chalk stick, just drooling at the mouth that they'll get their quota for the day working against the working people of the city.

No one cares though. Everyone is rushing and dealing with their own rat race.

With a filled daily schedule, I won't be able to leave the classroom to move my car. So, I sit in my car to come up with ideas of how to solve this problem. If I don't move my car I'll be slapped with an $80 parking fee. My day rate is about $120. I've paid $5 to cross the bridge and more money to pay for gas, car maintenance, insurance and tires. I need a brake job soon, but that will have to wait. My car is old and maintenance is going to get more expensive but I certainly can't buy a new car. And public transportation? I couldn't even get to most of these jobs by bus.

These thoughts whiz through my head. I'm not coming up with any good answers. I had circled the neighborhood for blocks and blocks to find a better spot. So, I continue to ponder my options and I begin to imagine the confrontation with a meter maid. Ah, another low wage earner! There are many of us. I see a scenario play out with her look of wry. "Give YOU a break? I'm a meter maid who has to make my quotas!" as she slaps me with a ticket. There's a stand off - a substitute teacher whose presumable parking ticket will cost a near full day's wage! No! I'm trying to get ahead! No, I'm just trying to tread water - PG&E, college loan which will not go away for 30 years. I'll be dead by then!

I see the little shits, the nerds going off to their downtown scene with free sandwiches and fooseball escapades, those techies making $300,000 and up. The nerds have taken over, those with no social skills and no concern for humanity. They are tied to their little machines. That's how I feel right now. Remember them in high school? They were the weird ones who lacked grace or even a capacity to look up from their tinkering. They laughed at the rest of us when tech world emerged and suddenly their little tinkering gadget transformed into a hot rod car and sexy girlfriend and left us all speechless. Films were even made about it.

Or, the doctors in their fancy houses and cars. Don't we have the formula wrong? Don't we want to invest in the early years so we don't end up having doctors cash out on ill people? Dietary diseases with obesity, diabetes and more are some of the worst killers in our country with medical systems cashing out in the billions on these people! Big fancy hospitals as temples displayin the diseased system we live in without just acknowledging if we educated kids well enough they wouldn't get sick with obesity, diabetes, mental healthy issues and more! Our system is toxic, upsidee down and backwards.

I want to scream again. I look at the homeless on the streets, lost, sad and forgotten. San Francisco used to have a heart. What has happened to this beautiful city I loved?

At mid day, she got me. The meter maid. $79 - a half a day's wage. What does a working person do in this town?

"A Ticket. They got me" I told the school office administration.

"I am so sorry. Here, I can split it with you.." He starts to pull out two twenties from his OWN wallet.

"No no, I can't accept that. That's okay. But why don't teachers get passes?" I ask, in hopes of solving a problem for future teachers.

"Yeah, you can get permits. They cost $140," he says.

I think of the amount of time and paperwork it would take to get those permits. I don't have time! I'm just in survival mode! Shouldn't such permits be sent to me with a ribbon around a box, a welcome package to substitute teachers with a note - "we know you are entering a world of hell, but we want you to know we at least value you. A parking pass you can call your own!"

Even The Monopoly game has Free Parking.

"That's a full day's wage. Really?" I'm nearly at a loss for words.

No, I'm in shock. What kind of city does this to TEACHERS? Clearly they are wiping out all the smart people because what smart person would do this to themselves? The city that once was a force for the intellectual, supporting artists, writers and those who had vision. Yet, it has become toxic, the city that I once loved. The city that I still love.

"I"ll fight it. What do you think the chances are?" I ask the school administrator.

He shakes his head. I'll take it straight to Pelosi, I think. Her and her entourage of fancy cars. Nancy Pelosi, the officiate for the marriage ceremony of billionaire oil heiress Ivy Getty. Pelosi, the Neoliberal Queen herself. Pelosi, the Speaker of the House.

No, I'll be the speaker for what's become insanity. It is insanity.

November, 2020. Marin County.

"Keep him on task." My instructions again.

He was a wiggly boy with blue hair. He just wanted to keep moving his fingers. I had him in a room the prior week and I really liked him. A quirky kid, an artist type who really had his own ideas and his own way of wanting to do them, which clearly did not fit into the system's way, so no one knew what to do with him. The teacher couldn't attend to him fully so she settled with his intention to tie knots to keep him busy. And, yes, he made beautiful sophisticated knots that would have the best sailors impressed.

All the students had their laptops open and were looking at something. But this one boy would not stare long enough to whatever the other kids were staring at. He kept changing from one Youtube to another despite anything I tried to do to keep him on track.

"They are watching!" he pointed to an icon on his computer. I looked up to the teacher and he looked at me. Indeed, the teacher could plug into his computer to see what he was looking at. He was under surveillance by the teacher! He was being conditioned to accept the idea of being under surveillance! When did this begin to happen in our schools? We are teaching this to our children - that they can be watched by authority and there is nothing they can do about it.

This is NOT education.

A chill went through my body. My God. This is what we are teaching our children in this toxic era of neoliberalism, on the bring of total technology domination in our schools and everywhere in our lives. We must end it before it's too out of control.

There was no paper in the classroom. Only laptop computers, buttons, files . . . and apps. I had a hard time even following how to get to the website page for the kids, to write about plate tectonics. The kids hated it too, yet they were required on this page to write down what they knew.

The Aftershock of Neoliberal Education

The student who had to stay on task has the blank screen, with nothing typed. I asked him about his answers for plate tectonics.

"Don't care. Don't care." And he pushes the "Submit."

At least he showed honesty.

Then immediately he want onto a youtube and fell into a cooking show about scrambled eggs. He put his face up inches away from the screen and was sat mesmerizing for several minutes as eggs got scrambled. What the hell?

"Come on, your teacher said you could watch an origami program and do your paper art." I try my best to encourage him.

"I get ideas from this too," he said.

Then he switched the program to violent gun action.

"We can't watch this. It's totally inappropriate." I say.

I like guns and explosives and dangerous things, though." he answers.

"How about frogs!" I knew an origami frog project. You have to work with what you got.

"I don't like frogs."

"Oh, but frogs can be very dangerous. You know about poisonous frogs?"

In that moment I started making an origami frog from the paper in my own backpack. He was watching pretending not to show interest, but I had him. For at least five minutes.

November 2019, San Francisco

"They are really disrespectful," the teacher's support said to me.

I liked her right away. A mere twenty year old out of Bayview, San Francisco, an area known for its financial and levels of inequity. She was hard on herself.

"I mean, I should have listened more when I was a kid. But I'm leaning as this class is learning." she said to me with humility.

I liked her. Really liked her. She was taking responsibility for her own education, recognizing her own lack of education she got in school, partly due to her own responsibility. That was noble, I thought. Mature and it inspired me. As a young adult she wanted to be educated. She would be a powerhouse one day, I thought.

When I walked into the room she had hustled to write down on the white board instructions, in a way to show that she cared about what she was doing. I made her nervous in the beginning, I could tell. She saw me as an authority and wanted to be recognized as doing her job well. Funny thing about that was I saw her being more of an authority than me! She knew the kids and besides, I was just the lowly substitute. And that told me more about her - that she does care and wants to do a really great job. That I respect.

The kids poured into the room with so much noise, hitting each other and kicking chairs. I could see the trouble makers right away, those desperate for attention in this attention deficit disordered world we live in where the teacher has no time to give attention to any single student.

I was getting prepared to stand my ground and show up as a strong adult who cared which also has its downside that they'll think I'm bossy, authoritarian and a bitch. The world is not perfect. What to do?

A skate punk pummeled in with his skateboard. I then recalled what I learned from Captain Richard, a sailing instructor who would take hardened inner city school kids sailing on the San Francisco Bay. He had once said to me to find the nastiest, meanest one of the bunch and make him the example. I asked the punk kid's name, took no bullshit and put a stack of papers in his hands. "Go distribute these please." This next hour would be survival for me.

A young black youth wouldn't come in. He was fussing about how he looked in the reflection on the door's window. Tying his tie. When I approached him to ask him to sit down as he was creating a distraction for the rest of the kids, he said. "Why would you want to be a teacher anyway?"

"I like kids and education is important," I answered.

He winced at me and then sauntered in. He pulled out his chair as all the students watched him. He was king in this class and he wanted to show me his power.

He was nothing but a middle school thug, and it kills me to say that. I can spot them right away when they enter. The strut, the ego, the look at me and how they choose to sit down. It will be a power war. How much he or she can control the classroom and make me as small as possible in order to maintain their social power at the school, their kingdom until they're an adult and realize the real world where no one cares. To balance perhaps abuse they get home or on the streets. They will find glory in merely disrupting me as I take attendance. And they get away with it.

He started to terrorize another kid, and I stepped toward him to intervene. I used my authoritarian approach which only elevated his defiance. I looked across the room for back up, from the support teacher in the room. She shook her head, as a message to me to stop approaching the thug. I took her cue figuring there was more to the story then I knew. I walked away from him. And he smiled, another moment when he won a battle with a teacher.

The support teacher came to me later. "He's one of those special kids. The last sub got into a screaming match with him which ended in disaster."

I couldn't believe she was wanting to coddle a thug. My God. What about the other kids in the classroom?

The class went on and as the kids did the work, the thug got up and walked around. He figured I couldn't do a thing to him. On the back wall was a collection of artwork from the students, stories of their heritage. I started to read them and the thug passed me by.

"Are one of these yours?" I asked him. He looked at them but didn't reply. I pointed to an Irish story. "This is like my story, my family story. See, the Irish came on ships and had been starving to death, following the potato famine. The wealthy landlords were kicking them out for not paying after their crops spoiled. They had no where to go but America. And nobody liked them. They found them to be dirty and uneducated."

He stopped in that moment listening to me. There was a connection, albeit a brief one. The support teacher came up to me a bit later. "I have never seen him connect with a teacher like I saw him connect with you. What were you saying to him?"

"I just told him my own family story about abuse, exploitation and hunger."

When do we end the abuse, I want to know? When do the oppressed stop becoming the oppressor? When can we view power and control as distasteful instead of glorious? When can we become humble and recognize we are mere humans on a big spinning ball in the middle of a mysterious universe?

It was a short time later the announcement came on. It was a call for a school shut down. Close windows, doors and get into lock down mode.

My God.

The entire class hustled into position, under tables, into the corner, closing windows.

I couldn't lock the door. I didn't have the key.

The terror that runs through you is unbelievable. I didn't know whether it was a drill or for real. Is there a shooter at the school? We all listened to the footsteps. There was a sound outside by the window, which weren't closed. My God. What would happen in this class dynamic if there was a sure sense of danger? Would we help one another? I don't know. I didn't want to find out. The thug kid even squatted down though it also appeared he was ready to take on a fight. In that moment, I wondered if he'd actually become the hero in such a scene, a kid ready for a good fight. I'd want him on my team.

Finally, all was fine, but it wasn't. We were all jolted and there was no changing that energy. The class was done. There was no learning. And they left when the bell rang, completing another day of school.

October 2019. San Francisco

The class would be a challenge. Already a single room packed with kids who clearly did not want to be in the class, mixed with kids who gave me lip about being white. I understand anger, so I just tried to show kindness and be supportive, the best I could. It'd be a challenge and I was ready.

I started to call out names for roll, when suddenly machine gun firing went off near the open window. I turned quickly toward it with a snap of my neck? Was that for real? Is it coming from outside?. I suddenly had my suspicions and my years of radio sound work was paying off for me. I knew it was a recording.

A young black girl was sitting close to the window so I naturally looked at her.

She seemed uneasy as I looked at her but I wasn't accusing her. I was looking at her because she was close to the origin of the sound. She was a beautiful black young student, shy and clearly set aside from all the other kids for some special reason that I didn't know. I tried to be gentle. And given a race war was happening in the classroom, me a white bitch who is in a spot of authority with kids ready to smack me down if I hint at anything racist, I asked if she'd help me by handing out the papers. She did and then in moments she disappeared from the class.

Machine gun firing again. And then music. What the hell? Was it coming from outside? I looked out the open window. Stupid? Would the school get me on that one, not following protocol when there is gun fire? Was it a set up to test me as a teacher about school protocol? But then again it didn't sound real. The students watched me. Was it a joke on me?

I refused to flinch. I held my grace like a steel rod, if a steel rod had grace.

I asked another girl about the missing one who had been passing out paper. "Do you know where she went?" I asked nicely, or as nice as I could.

"You made her cry! That's what you did!"

What? What did I say and what did I do to be accused of making her cry?

At that point I got on the phone to call the office. I was worried about her. Where did she go? I was worried about gun fire in the classroom. I was worried about mutiny. I was worried that I'd lose my job, be fired and arrested for something! I was worried about not making my rent and paying for food for my kids. I was worried about losing my kids! I was worried I was losing my wits! And I had to keep my cool, act professional and solve the problem.

The three girls got up, gang like, walked toward me and then veered and walked out the door.

"Where are you going? Please come back." I said.

They didn't.

A man was sitting outside in the hall, like one would in a prison. "I'll call security", he said.

"Security? At a school?" I said. I was learning. Security.

Moments later security came with the kids and meanwhile the shooting recording was found. Behind my back a kid went to retrieve it and I turned just in time to see him taking it from the radiator below the window. I approached him and put out my hand without a single word. Sheepishly he put it into my palm. Meanwhile, security was talking to the girls and an administrator arrived. I held out the recording device and machine gun firing went off.

"Would you like this?" I handed the device to the administrator.

The administrator looked embarrassed, took it and said nothing more. There was no back up for me. Girls were sent back into the classroom and I was assumed to continue on teaching.

The three girls approached me and shouted in my face. "You called security. That's raw. You are a horrid, fucking bitch. A white fucking bitch!"

I kept my cool. "You will not speak to me that way" I used my poker face. I was getting good at this.

The Aftershock of Neoliberal Education

Keeping my cool. Meanwhile, half the class missed out on most of the lesson because of the bad behavior of a few kids. And to them I was sorry.

I hand wrote the incident on a piece of paper and gave it to the school as I left, just in case they needed it, for their records. There was no apology, there was no recourse. Nothing. Most schools, perhaps, would have called the culprits with explosion. In fact, I recall at my daughter's middle school in Marin, a boy was caught on camera by a sassy girl who was prodding him for saying something about bringing a gun to school. The entire school was shut down, parents were called. The sheriff arrived. The boy was expelled. He was actually a pretty gentle young man without a lot of friends. But here, in this hood, I was beginning to understand that if you follow that route each time, you risk funding. You risk kudos for your school. You have to come clean that your school is out of control. And that is not an easy task for anyone to come clean with, especially when your job relies on the insanity - school counselors, funding, teachers and administrators. What do you do?

Next time, I know what I'll do if I hear a recording device shoot off gun fire. I'll prop my feet up on the desk, pull out my phone and call the FBI. I'll hold a conversation about the perpetrators, all of them, in the classroom, and that I have the door locked and for the FBI to come and arrest the whole class.

Now, THAT would have gotten their attention and taught them a thing or two!

I'd keep my poker face and maybe they'd learn some respect.

We are missing respect. And we need adults to step up to show our children what unity looks like Where are the adults?

September 2019. San Francisco

I sat quietly eating my lunch of last night's cold dinner. I listen to youth outside. A few students enter the classroom during the lunch half hour.

"Can we sit in here?"

I thought it'd be fine until a lunch duty teacher walked in and told them to get out. I thought the kids would be nice enough but I was also having hard core lessons on the job, about what was acceptable and what wasn't.

I asked the teacher if everything was okay.

"Yeah, it's fine. I just have to pee," the male teacher said to me as he left. It was added visual I really didn't need to hear. I mean, could he have said I need to use the washroom . . . or the bathroom. But "pee." I imagine his hand. . . . oh, stop it Barbara! Everything just feels so rough and raw. Where is respect and dignity and grace?

I sat down at the desk with the left drawer open. It was packed solid with paper airplanes, confiscated hall passes, and broken pencils. I pulled out my reusable bamboo utensils, trying to feel I was doing something good for the world. Something. I felt like I was failing on all fronts.

The day had been brutal and I was only half way through it.

The bell rang and class was about to begin. I was at the ready for a stream or, in this case, a rush of students. And then they came.

A girl came in rough. She started knocking down chairs along the way, screaming her head off.

"Fuck, you can't even deal with your own shit!" she screamed at a thirteen year old girl with bright red hair and a red hot attitude. She decided to take her anger out on me within minutes. And then she sat down with a huff.

Fortunately I had already called security the moment she had walked in screaming and throwing chairs, as she was getting into a fight with a boy who was ready to get me fired for being white.

He had walked in early when I had asked him to pull out his work.

"Did you just tell me that you were going to sell me? Are you being a bully because I have black skin?" he said loud enough for everyone to hear.

He's been taught a lot. How do I tell him that I'm there for him? I did my best to be calm, speaking to him gently and respectfully. He quieted for the moment but didn't take out the work. He just sat in the back with his friends.

The vice principal arrived. Things had settled a bit. He asked, with intention, how I was doing.

"Well, the one boy and his friends sitting in the back aren't doing work. They are just sitting there," I say to the vice principal, who I had respect for.

"Take it. You're doing good," he said.

I could see this vice principal was doing what he could. But how do you manage so much anger? How do you give when a person isn't interested in accepting? How do you teach when simple civility isn't practiced? How do you say sorry for years of history when I wasn't even alive. . . and I'm doing my best as a human being to be a stand for doing the right thing? What is the right thing anymore? I really don't know.

If I choose NOT to come to these schools to substitute, I'm called a racist. If I come to the schools, I get abused and called a racist. There is no answer except we all must stop hating each other!

I had no time for the quiet, studious kids who wanted to learn and so I felt like a failure. The best I could do was leave a note for the teacher the names of the kids who were great, a small power I have as a substitute teacher. A validation for the kids who want to learn and are respectful. This is not school. This is survival.

November 2021, Marin County

I'm watching a fleet of buses come down the avenue toward the school. It's a new day in one of the most elite school districts of Marin County. I put my hat on as the PE Sub.

We play cone guardian. Why do we play cone guardian? I view it as one of the most violent games for children. Why do we teach children violent games, those that benefit the strong bully kids, not the sweet, gentle ones who cringe and feel lesser than they should because they don't like to show off muscle, speed and power?

Three girls got hurt. The bully, physically strong kids stood tall.

I look around at the school, looking for answers. Where are they?

Then the answer comes. A bugle plays from a loudspeaker. Time to change classes. A bugle? A military style bugle? At a school?

Why the competition? Why the army like posturing? Bells whistling? Straight lines marching from class to class? It's NOT natural. No, it's a set up to cultivate military minds of strength and domination. War is horrid and unnatural as much as people like to believe it is natural. Slaughtering people is NOT natural. And I'm sure you can ask most war veterans with missing arms and legs today that question and they would tell you WHY we shouldn't have wars.

Later I watch a group of girls play with hula hoops and think of the Native American hoop dance. Wouldn't it be more valued to tie in the sacred with the physical? Music, performance, dance, circus arts - JOY! Is this a type of beauty that we have somehow admonished so we can cater to the bullies? I think of so many creative arts including tight ropes, slack lines, trampolines . . instead of all these games involving balls, competition, physical muscles and force.

Our schools benefit the bullies. We create and sanction bullies. This has been the education. This is who we have become.

It's finally lunchtime. To be civilized! I think of the Guatemalan and Italian culture, two I'm fairly familiar with. I think how food brings such unity, sitting together, talking and enjoying life when people can pause from all their activity, join a table, eat together and talk.

In Rome years ago I watched a group of about twenty children eat with glee the most beautiful food that was carefully set out on a big table - homemade pasta, prosciutto, cheeses, risotto and other traditional Italian dishes hot from the oven. How excited the children were. They didn't rush to finish the meal. Instead they were part of the experience of expectation – to sit together, talk and enjoy, just as the grown ups were doing. Their meal lasted a long time and I thought how civilized the young children were, understanding healthy food rather than rushing for the sweets, which were almost healthy too, with apples, figs and other fruits instead of colored frosting, artificially colored candy with or other sugary foods that serve absolutely zero nutrition.

But, alas. Here I am in my own country and I stand in horror. Packaged foods, sugar laden snacks. Pizza. Chicken nuggets. Sugary drinks. I scan for nutrition, good food. I find some but not a lot. They don't sit. They don't talk, They yell and scream. But, it's so loud that in order to be heard one has to scream, which supports the loud antagonistic children instead of the quiet, reserved ones who sit in silence. The teachers all stand around either eating or blowing their whistle. Trash falls to the ground, packages of Dorritos, fruit strips, pretzels.

If we don't show children how to simply be civilized and sit at a table quietly with respect and value the very singular action that not only nourishes their body and mind, how to we survive as a society? The very core of schooling should be how to sit with respect with one another. Talk and listen to one another with respect. To value food for its nutrition and where it comes from, having a deep relationship with that process. It's the underpinning of our entire civilized world!

Such is not an elite action and should never be construed as such. But who are we, as adults in this nation, to teach our children this when we don't even abide by these actions ourselves? Who sits together at night with families in a civilized way and talk about the day? I don't even do that and yet I remember a time in my life I did and those are some of my richest memories. My former German mother in law serving me homemade gnocchi fresh from her kitchen. An arugula salad grown in the backyard of my former Italian father in law. Candles lit. A napkin placed just in the right place. A family discussion about the right way to set a table. Everything was so simple, but then it wasn't. A daily ritual to stop and think about life together and to share experiences, ideas face to face while enjoying beauty together. It's a bonding mechanism that we have at our ploy. . . and it should NEVER be construed with elitism. It's a basic human act.

When I ran for the school board in my county a few years back, I chose to be radical which really didn't mean much other than challenging the status quo. I spoke about changing the football fields, a game that promotes male toxicity into gardens to feed the school, an act that would help youth grow a direct relationship to soil and our food, the very grounding of health and life. They laughed at me. I went so far as even suggesting our schools take on abused animals as a sanctuary to help students learn how to nurture, connect with life cycles and heal. That one got a real good laugh! But, I was actually serious. But, the one that drew anger was when I suggested high school students be mandated to go on a field trip to a slaughter house to witness the actions of killing an animal for our food. If this is part of our system, why do we not share this truth with our children? I nearly jolted the entire system with that suggestion.

We had an earthquake drill mid morning. After all classes were evacuated, I imagined something else. How to drill for war. I feel it coming. I looked up to the sky. What would we do if the jets were here and not in Syria? We are living in a very dangerous time as more truths get unraveled and we have to stop and look at one another with who and what we have been. It's uncomfortable.

A helicopter circles around. They are flying low to inspect powerless around neighborhoods to ensure fire safety. We've endured so many fires these past years in nearby counties, entire communities going up in flames. We are at great risk in my community, one that is surrounded by nature, open lands. It feels like a ticking bomb, or war. And how do we drill for that?

November 2019, San Francisco

It's 5am. My flip phone alarm goes off with a shrill. Why doesn't anyone come up with soft spoken words like my mom used to use when waking me up for school. Maybe there's a business plan in that and it'll make me a million dollars. It's an idea!

"Sweetie, rise and shine! Wake up, honey. Time to say goodbye to dream land. You've got a fucking crazy world to go deal with so go power up on some oatmeal and coffee!"

Well, it wasn't exactly like that, but you get my point.

I shift myself on the lumpy sofa and realize I hadn't bought almond milk for my coffee. I'm out of sugar - the noose is tightening. All the good immediate reasons to get out of bed are nonexistent. This is what survival feels like. Step by step luring to get you to move forward because the big picture of it all is way too much and unappealing.

I pull the blanket over my head. Ten more minutes of peace before this new day, one which requires a one hour drive into San Francisco during the dark hours of the morning, ironically into a neighborhood where my ex-husband and I had lived together, the better years and I earned a decent living as a thirty year old and lived in a great Victorian home with my whole life ahead of me. Now, I'm fifty three years old making almost the same amount of money I did as a college student, while working with a Master's Degree and its debt in our public schools. I'll spend a day as a sub getting kicked around, hopefully without getting a parking ticket this time.

I sip my bitter black coffee. I think about the idea of giving up coffee. If I gave up coffee I wouldn't feel denied of pleasure at the moment. I decide to do it. It's my last sip of bitterness. I'm giving it up. And I'm ready to be vigilant for one more day.

After the full day of work, I'll have to drive the four to five hours, likely with traffic, to pick up my thirteen year old son who I have not seen for over one month. As his mother, I feel I have missed out on his entire childhood and it hurts me deeply that these circumstances have separated me from my own blood. I curse my ex husband every day of my life. . . and his girlfriend. . . . I hope one day women will start sticking together instead of sabotaging mothers. How can a woman walk into a relationship so fast and take over MY DUTIES as a mother? She's a thief and a liar. Had she had some self respect, she would have looked at the man straight in the face and said "dude, go figure yourself out and take a stand for your wife and family! BE A MAN!" But, instead she plops her clothes into my closet next to my wedding dress and gets cozy in MY bed that I bought and assembled while I was six months pregnant with my dear great aunt's chest at the foot of the bed. Some women need hard reminders of what it means - to be a sister in this world of sisterhood. I have no problem calling her out.

It's the problem with money. As a person herself who doesn't have money, folks look for the next best deal, even sabotaging their sisters. It's been a 2000 year way of doing business, sadly, as women have failed to stand up for each other in this male powered moneyed world. It needs to change.

But, I do my best not to cater to anger and hate. It's bad for the soul.

"Get counseling, Barbara. Deal with your emotions," my ex had said to me the last time.

No, I have a better plan, thank you very much.

October, 2019, Marin County

I had a new idea for a dissertation "Education Under the Age of Neoliberalism - A Lesson Plan for Fascism. "

I'll include "Leadership models" which encourage bullying as the precept of leadership. Leadership is a means of getting people to do what you want them to do, as that does seem to be how leadership is now defined in practice. I'll include expensive classes that you can "buy." and earn certificates to show how great you are, except we already have those with Yale and Harvard.

I'll create fancy names with paid for classes so people can ooh and aah when they see someone has a certificate from these classes, a sure sign of their greatness and why you should listen to them.

My Irish family culture is rising inside me, the rebellious finger to the establishment and money people, the spirit that got the Irish through the British occupation, and likely still does given England still owns half of Ireland. As I think about my own life choices, I was the one in my family who failed. I wanted to go to college, a sell out. My grandfather and uncles prided themselves for not spending a day in college.

"Why would you want to sit in a room all day and have someone tell YOU what to think and how to think. Go figure that out yourself!" I remember the words so vividly. My grandfather was a self made engineer. He designed and built airplanes, his passion, in his garage while he acted like a mailman during the day to pay for his passion. Stanford engineers would come to his home and marvel at his designs and ask how he did it.

"Commonsense," he'd say. And later he'd tell us, those with fancy degrees have lost all their commonsense.

We have pictures of him smiling high in the sky, flying his Keleher Lark, as he named it. He smiled big, because no one owned him. No university could claim his brilliant accomplishment, feeding themselves credit. He did it on his own and gets to claim the glory.

I hear the students outside walking, shouting, laughing and running. The bell rings. I sit alone in a quite a class room all alone. I have no class this hour. I have no internet to escape to.

I look at a book sitting behind the teacher's desk. "Developing Expert Learners" by Michael McDowell. I pick it up and start reading, an old fashion action that I miss deeply. I read.

"As educators, we are challenged to prepare our students for college and career readiness as they go into the real world."

They are part of the real world! Duh! I want to scream! It's not education. It's classroom management- yelling, pride, ego, photos, narcism. Why do we want to feed an unhealthy society? No, we should be teaching them how to create their own society dictated by the ideas of grace, dignity, honesty and justice and show them how to live it instead of acting disgraceful and preaching it to them!

Schools mascots are animals like the cougar or bulldog - all fierce and aggressive. Where is the grace?

I never asked for this in my life. "Don't tell me what to be!" I screamed long ago to the world.

And here I am that person. That teacher behind a desk. What is my responsibility other than telling the kids to run for their lives? That's how I feel on some days.

October 2019, San Francisco County

Diane Feinsten School. I'm in my old San Francisco neighborhood. The Sunset District. It's where I found my soul for the first time, sitting on a beach and watching the waves, washing away my own early schooling indoctrination. Asking the ocean and sky big questions about spirituality, meaning of life and my future. I was in my early twenties, trying to figure out the world and where I would fit in. Funny. The answer to those questions still allude me. I'm yearning to return to San Francisco. I have to finish Marin County, though, I think. It will tell me when it's time. San Francisco has changed so much. It's becoming mechanical, technical and dangerous as big tech has dominated the landscape with coding and systems displacing the heart of the rebel Bohemians who listened to poetry, danced with music and laughed about absurdities.

The Aftershock of Neoliberal Education

Diane Feinstein, a Senator. A US Senator worth $120 million with her investment husband. She was filmed with a group of children recently telling them they know nothing about what to do about climate change when it's been Feinstein's career legacy that has led us to it. I miss the Bohemians. They would laugh at this absurdity and write a fantastic poem about it akin to *The Howl*. Now I enter a school of her namesake, a kindergarten class. The folks of the school are very nice. What's not nice is having to enter the schools with portraits of Diane Feinstein hanging on the wall commemorationg her years in office. I close my eyes as I walk past them and take a deep breath. I can do this.

In this kindergarten class, there is one teacher and twenty three students. Two of the children are out of control, bless their little hearts. They are the last stand and standing strong not to conform. Little Billy reminds me of my son when he was little, but more extreme - he literally runs around out of control.

"Just let him run" says his Para.

I think of Helen Keller before her teacher came, how she ran around at the dinner table until her teacher gave her a firm lesson and taught her how to speak and listen. The other students watched little Tony and some decided to mimic.

"If he can do it. . . why not me?" I hear them think. At least the children follow logic. You have to admire them for that.

It's hard not to become authoritarian or want to shout. It's a kindergarten class and I must remember they are a mere five years out of the womb. I do think back to those teachers who screamed and shouted at those in other kindergarten classes, forcing them into silent obedience and fear. That wasn't right either.

A teacher in charge of twenty three students in a singular classroom. Or cell.

After getting the kids settled, I have a three minute point of calm where I can talk about the sound of "s" and "m" and give instructions.

Little Billy screams hurting all our ears. And it takes time to recover.

Later, after lunch, Tony disappeared. We were merely walking back from the cafeteria as a long snake, one by one in a line, like they do in military camps and school grounds. It's a sign of a good teacher. How straight the line is behind you. I'm trying my best.

We returned to the classroom, the kids put down their backpacks without incident and sat down. I marveled at myself. I accomplished such greatness in that moment. I had a little wee bit of an accomplished act that day to feed me the next hours. I stand and admire the students with that feeling of being a great teacher. Until. . .

Where is Tony? His chair is empty. But he was in line. He was part of the long snake! Where did he go? My mind bursts into worry and uncertainty. I have a missing child. But, how do I leave a room of twenty two children to find one little escape artist who managed to cut loose between the lunch room and the class room?

On cue, Little Miles starts screaming. "There's a spider in the room!" Mayhem breaks loose and the sweet little souls who had made me so proud, jump off their seats to see the scary spider.

I pull out my defense. "STICKERS!"

"Who wants a sticker?" I say with half pleading and charm with a hint of authoritarism. It's a cocktail that only some teachers are clever enough to create . . . we do sell this secret for a price. I think. We have to survive too. A spider. Missing Billy. Tiger stickers. This is my life in this moment of insanity.

A Para walks in. "Where's Tony?"

"Not here." I say with probable guilt. How do you tell anyone that a child under your care who you had just walked from the lunchroom to the classroom disappeared without looking or sounding like a fool.

"Probably the cafeteria or the bathroom. He practiced a Houdini act as we walked back," I answer.

She goes on the Billy hunt. While I go on the spider hunt.

The Para and Tony arrive within minutes. He is out of sorts. He's crying and not wanting to listen to me or to her. Meanwhile, it's time to get the other kids lined up for the library. Billy says he wants to come too and he joins us a newly created snake line to the library through the halls and I keep one eyeball on him all the way.

When we arrive to the library quietly, Billy heads straight for the furniture to jump on it like a trampoline and starts throwing the pillows.

I look for help from the The Librarian. She just stands shaking her head and says to me "that's Billy, bless his little heart." I see she has love in her heart for his little guy. I share that love with her and just want to hug little Billy to say that I wish I had all the time in the world for him because he is going to be one of those special people in the world who will defy all the crap that we've created. He's got a good heart and I can see that. He's just standing his ground - He wants to be a kid and out of as system that is truly unhealthy. You have to admire him for that.

Billy erupts on our way back in the hallway. Another teacher comes out and we hold Tony and he screams and thrashes. I have twenty two other children who are all sitting and waiting for us, time missed with them in order to deal with one child who I have to care for in this moment. It's only me. The sub. The lowly sub. After about fifteen minutes of thrashing and screaming Tony comes into the classroom quietly.

Later I do have a quiet moment with Tony. I present him three balls and show him how to juggle. To my surprise he starts to pick it up, even better than me, which, in true honesty, I'm not very good at it. I read about these techniques, to use your hands to help crosswire your brain and it's a calming method, especially for people who have a lot of energy. Billy has a tremendous amount of energy and just because he can't sit like a robot in a classroom listening to a teacher and writing on worksheets does not indicate he lacks brilliance. In fact, his rebellion may demonstrate this child is gifted and we need to hold onto to Billy. Our school structure is set up in a singular way, absent from what is natural, along with natural play.

Kindergarten classes have become highly academic rather than joyful, socializing play based. Billy could show us a different way. I've talked to an adult dear friend of mine who was a lot like Billy when he was a kid. He got into a lot of trouble because of his big energy. Today my friend is a multi ton licensed captain for ships and has sailed throughout the world. He had one ship he captained and I crewed where we carried children to teach them about the great ocean, showing young rebellious boys how to hold the helm in winds of 30knots while the boat heeled hard. I witnessed a spark of life return to the eyes of those hardened boys, after likely years of having teachers and society tell them they know nothing. When you raise your own sails and navigate your boat with choices, a spirit grows. Our system doesn't support these kind of people. We squash them instead and tell them what to be and how to be.

Billy is a gift to all of us.

His mom picks him up she asks sheepishly. "How did he do?" I talk to her briefly and tell her some of the challenges. But I also talk to her about his gifts. "You have an amazing son. Hold him tightly." And I show her Little Tony's juggling act. She stands amazed. I smile.

November 2019. Marin County

I greet the high school students and give my ice breaker question. Who is Jimmy Carter?

Not a single high school student in this class knows the name "President Jimmy Carter." It blows my mind. How is that possible? How is it possible that an entire generation of youth have no inkling of an idea that there was a president, who happens to still be alive, who likely had the biggest impact on their generation? A president who tried to stop climate change and got smashed by a generation of baby boomers? It is by far the greatest story of our age, the level of propaganda that not only got embedded in media but also our educational institutions, propaganda driven education that emboldens the billionaires and those who have exploited the people versus those who actually stood up for the people?

I have to take a minute to center myself. This is so much bigger than little me.

There is a lot of talk about about presidents and orange hair. At least they are currently politically minded.

"Why do these leaders have such ugly hairstyles?" one kid asks me.

"Well, when you're 70 years old we'll look at you and what style you got!" I answer with a laugh.

Still, it's the loud ones who get the attention. The quiet kids keep their heads low, listen and do their work. They don't complain, they just accept the fact that they get shut down and that's the way it is.

Fidgets. Does it really make them more nervous? What about old fashion doodling? Can they lean not on a gadget or are we just caving into cultivating bad habits? There is a whole drawer full of gadgets in the teacher's desk, objects that spin, pop and whiz. Why do they need to fidget so much?

I wonder. What has happened to the idea of training oneself, especially a student, to rise to a better self with self discipline and practice? Oh, right, the teachers just need to get through an assignment because that is how a teacher will be judged . . . and his or her job depends on it. We are failing.

I'm feeling my oats today. I tell the students that I'm not a "sub." They grow quiet, unsure of who I am. I can see their little minds whizzing and trying to figure me out as they watch me carefully.

"I am a leadership coach," I say. While standing up tall and throwing my shoulders back in full self confident stance. I look at them individually, as if I am now the one watching them.

Their demeanor changes. This has been a little test of mine, a little subversive trick.

"Which students can show me who is a leader and help guide a productive class? I take notes for your teacher and I like to write down the names of those who help guide the class."

That trick worked well today. I got through it. There are leaders.

November 2019, San Francisco County

I try to help one student in a very loud classroom. Kids will not quiet down. It's like a mob scene all contained in a little room like an insane asylum. That's really what it looked like . . . and felt like. I mean, what do I do? Send them all to the principal's office? Hog tie them? Writing names on the board will not work, it'll just bring a smile to their faces, a recognition that they got attention for the day.

I see some quiet students upset by the noise, covering their ears. Who came up with this crazy idea to shove a bunch of adolescent kids into a day long cycle of going in and out of classrooms to be fed propaganda?

That's what it feels like, but I can't think about that. Not yet.

Are any doing their work? One girl looks like she's falling out of her chair, or is she being silly or needing attention? That was my first read. She pulls out her lipstick as I squat next to her to help her get back on track.

"Isn't it pretty" she says about the lipstick and then starts talking about her social life.

I gently stop her and point her in the direction of her text book, the reading required for the day. But she is indifferent. She's looking around the classroom completely distracted, of course. Who wouldn't be? It's a circus!

Suddenly she squeals and with wide eyes looks right at me. "Look what I can do!"

She has muscles on her temples that I did not know existed on humans. Her entire forehead shifts back and forth. Her eyes pop out. I have never seen a human being contort their face in such an incredible way. I'm trying not to be grossed out but on some level I'm captivated by the marvels of the human body. I try to stay positive and professional.

"Hmm, you have talent!"

Then I turn back to the book, to bring her attention to the mass slaughter in our country's history, with images of Indigenous people and black people and wars.

She blurts out again. "Look, I can also do this!" I look.

Her shoulder becomes disjointed and she moves it around in a way that creates a loud cracking sound, louder than the noise in the classroom. I have never seen in my life a contortionist, which she clearly is. If I were at Circus d'Soleil I'd be clapping loudly! If she were performing a dance with a fanciful dress using her talents on the stage of Carnegie Hall she'd be rich and famous. But, because she is sitting at a desk in an institution that should be impounded she's deemed to be an unruly student who can't focus and should be sent to the counselor's office and haver her parents called so they can all address her unruly behavior? How do we teach under these circumstances?

I acknowledge another amazing talent she surely has. I try to lure her back to the text book because as a teacher I'm judged by how much she will follow me by reading the horrors of our American history. The bison are now being slaughtered.

She looks at me.

"But then THIS is my special move!" She blurts out with more excitement than ever.

She literally falls out of her chair, collapsing onto the floor in a moment's notice. She brings her right leg up, like a broken limb and rolls back her eyes like a posting on Facebook of the Zombie Apocalypse.

What do you say in that moment? What do you do in that moment? On a human level, you're simply blown away that a human being can actually act in such a manner. And I am human.

I was never trained in this capacity - how to stop a contortionist in the middle of history class examining our country's disjointed malice that has plagued us since its colonization? I do my best.

"Dear child, you have incredible talent," I say with all sincerity. Then I ask her politely to return to the book to read our great Constitution.

"We the People of the United States, in Order to form a more perfect Union, establish Justice, insure domestic Tranquility, provide for the common defence, promote the general Welfare, and secure the Blessings of Liberty to ourselves and our Posterity, do ordain and establish this Constitution for the United States of America."

I have transcended from being a teacher back into a human being. I am cracking myself. The bell rings and the contortionist readjusts here eyes and her legs, puts on her lipstick and bounces out the room into the world of this Great American society.

The room is quiet. It's lunch time. I sit alone at the wooden desk and take a bite of my sandwich after I try that temple forehead move she did so well . . . I'll never master that one.

November 2019, San Francisco County

Junk books. Why? I have brought the young children to a book fair in the library, apparently an attempt to inspire the kids to read. I peruse the books, all glitzy and sparkly. Where is the literature? These are junk books. I want to raise my hand and question how did we get to this point? But who will listen?

The books are vacant of what literature tried to deliver - stories to learn by, stories to celebrate our humanity or challenge our humanity. Literature. These are junk books. And haven't we learned yet given that nobody reads anymore that by shoving books down our children's throats as we recite the mantra "Read, read, read" that we are abusing them? It's true. We have lost the essence of what reading is all about and how stories can transform us.

The children get rewarded by how many books they read. Another example of consumeristic, neoliberal education. Who said the more books you read the smarter you'll be? Shouldn't we be focused on quality instead of quantity? Shouldn't we teach the students how to savor instead of exploit?

This mentality goes so deep into our current psyche and spills out onto our children. As I look at one pink glittery book with content I can't even remember, I recall Easter egg hunts which follow the same mentality. Take as many eggs you can get. Or Christmas where children are inundated with candy, sweets and toys. The sacredness of all these things have been bought out and replaced with big money and an intention that is not in line with that which is true.

Junk food, commercialized education, entertainment and books. Such is my observation today. I'm feeling overwhelmed once I tap into this feeling. Our innocent children are being groomed to be the next consumeristic society while adults cash out on them.

Our kids are the most vulnerable and easy to pillage population in our country. I'm reminded of a film I saw at a youth film festival. A young student filmmaker conducted an experiment with his cafeteria food. Could it decompose? The cafeteria food did not decompose. It didn't even mold. The food wasn't food. It was just a few DNA molecules away form being a lego. Okay, that was a joke, but then it wasn't.

People laughed at the film and somehow didn't rise in anger and injustice. THESE ARE OUR KIDS! It's as if childhood is a hazing opportunity. If you get through it, you've deserved to become an adult! We raise our children like coaches train football players, and you're either good and play the game or your out! When did that start?

The first week of the pandemic, our own schools in Marin County dished out Fruit Loops, Cocoa Puffs and Pop Tarts to the families . . . one of the most wealthy school districts in the country gave poison to our children. And people are not rising to this insanity? Where is sanity?

Our children are sacred and we abuse them, exploit them and treat them so horrifically in this society that we should have no surprises when one day they decide to treat others the same way.

We adults are failing our children. Our children are sacred.

November 2019, San Francisco

The new office secretary at the middle school is trying. She's young and she is trying. It's a lot to ask of any one person. She's trying her best. I see it.

She gives me the assignment, a key and room number. First, she shares with me a schedule for classes and then she changes it, giving me two one hour classes for the entire day. She sets me off at 8am and I am to return at 3:30 pm. That's it.

I walk up down the long empty corridor and then up the stairs inside the large school building. It's an old school and you can literally hear the voices from past decades, like whispering echoes of all the young lives who have walked this same halls. I reach the third floor and I look left and then right down the long empty corridor with dappled light coming from a few windows here and there. I walk slowly finding the classroom numbers. 301, 302, 305 . . . wait, what happened to the ones in-between? Finally I find my classroom. But the key isn't working. I have essentially ten minutes inside the classroom to review the class instructions for safety, curriculum, notes about students and schedule before the students arrive. I can't open the door. And the time is clicking away fast. Is it the key or is it me and my ability to use a darn key?

The neighbor teacher comes over and gives it the crank and the shimmy, along with a jerk. The door opens .

"It's temperamental," he says.

"Looks broken to me." I say with truth. I'm tired of falsehoods.

I find the desk in the back of the room specifically positioned so the teacher can watch the backs of the students. I read the instructions left on the desk for me, front and center. There have been times I have had no instructions. There have been times I've had to wander the classroom to find the instructions laying in an illogical place. But most often I also find the instructions to be like long lost letters. . . notes from the heart from one human to another. I know the teachers are tired and overworked. And with most of the instructions, they are indeed love letters, instructions to keep the students safe and happy while mixed with words of the teacher's exhaustion dealing with certain students.

I have five students in about seven minutes. I read the notes. "Keep all windows and doors closed and locked while they are in the classroom", I read. Is that a danger? Why would she write that, I wonder? What would the kids do if the windows were open? I'm on full alert. Five children tells me they are placed in this classroom because they need full attention as I sit behind them. Will they be violent? Sarcastic? What am I in for?

I'm prepared for the worst. It's just one hour after all. A one hour class.

The kids arrive. I quickly assess them but I don't note anything unusual about them. Normal kids. They sit and do their work. A couple of them are a bit like chatter boxes, but not malicious. Two of them are goofy. One has his head down and is working diligently. They are great kids. Why was I worried? Why was I warned to be worried?

I look at the window towards the Pacific Ocean, as the school sits on a high hill overlooking western part of San Francisco. In the horizon, I see a trail of smoke in the sky. I follow the trail with my eyes leading me to the coastal mountains of Marin County where I live. Suddenly I stiffen. Marin County is on fire. How big is the fire and how far is it from my home? After all these crazy California fires, many of which 30 year firefighter veterans have said straight to me, "I've never seen fires like this in my career," rapid, fast moving fires, we are all on alert and understand what fires can mean today - entire communities obliterated over night.

The Aftershock of Neoliberal Education

My daughter is at home sick for the day. I'm suddenly feeling a deep concern and worry. I get online quickly. The see there is a fire is in Geyservile, just north of us, a fire that is full throttle but this one looks closer . . and doesn't look right. A sense of panic fills me. I remain calm on the outside, using my poker face. But on the inside I'm gripped with fear. I text my daughter so she's on alert.

The next class begins and thirty screaming kids enter the classroom doing a great job to distract me from the fire concerns. I'm in the present moment again, full throttle survival. The kids come in out of control, obnoxious and rude.

"Is it like this all the time? I ask one calm kid. "Or, is this special for me?"

"Yes. It's always like this."

"I am so sorry." I say to her and I meant it.

When the bell rings to start the class and I begin taking roll, I get really get close to calm in the class. I play my "leadership" strategy with them, telling them that I'll write the names of kids who help us through the hour with respect and support.

"I love to share those names with the teacher," I tell them wholeheartedly.

A young girl approaches me. I understood with her scarf and limited English she is from the Middle East, Muslim, but I couldn't understood her words.

"I want to pray." she says through her Google app.

"Okay."

She takes her small carpet to a corner of the room and beings to pray, quietly. Other kids watch.

I think of the fire back in Marin . . . I get a text message. "It's been contained." My nerves are on edge. And I wouldn't mind praying too.

We are reading a story and I cannot remember the author. It's about a little girl who doesn't want to put her sweater on and the teacher is making her do so. The teacher is being made to look like the authoritarian in the story, the bad guy, for making the little girl put on her sweater. The story goes on with focusing on the child's determination to not want to wear it, making her the hero in the story. How do you teach as a teacher with such literature? With no respect for the teacher? We are sharing stories that focus on undermining the very people who are literally working piss wages to be on the child's team and to teach them? We are sabotaging ourselves as teachers pushing such literature! It's from a baby boomer, likely a story that shed the idea, as in the 60s, to rebel against all authority. But, when is enough enough? When are we kicking ourselves in the butt?

Perhaps there is value in the message of the story, to question authority. Okay, fine. But it would have been a far greater lesson to have shared the teacher's perspective, too! Maybe the child had a terrible history of losing the sweater - as most students do. The teacher was trying to teach the very sloppy child how to care for something instead of being disrespectful to an object that keeps you warm and someone took time to spend money on just for her! Just take a look at the piles of lost clothes in lost or found bins at schools. Perhaps it was cold outside. Perhaps the child needed to learn respect for a teacher. And more than that, when did we, as teachers, decide that it's proper for a young child not to listen to a trusted adult? The list could go on with another view point! The story was propaganda, pure propaganda! I mean, even Ronald Reagan nixed the Fairness Doctrine Ruling, nixing the other point of view that journalists were once required to write in order to share a proper story!

Indeed. This very story is an example of the neoliberal brainwashing building blocks, a mentality driven by the 60s movement, the same generation that fought against their own parents, standing up to any authority believing they were better, has undermined sensible and respectful teachers and ruined our schools!. That boomer generation had stood up to a generation who served in WW2 and either lost husbands, sons or brothers and that same boomer generation brought in the horrors of neoliberalism, The Reagan Era, as it should be called. I think about that idea of standing up to authority that a generation gave to us. And while it's always important to question authority, it's also important to respect different views. When do we make that call? And when do we stand up to the neoliberal/boomer generation? I'm ready!

We today face incredible history of 40 years of wars, economic inequality and climate crisis. This past same generation must face its own foes and its failures. A generation was defiant in the 60s as youth. As adults these last 40 years they have failed more than the society they stood up to back in the 60s. That's got to feel like a bitch. . . a lesson in life. Be careful when you criticize because it can come full circle and kick you in the butt. And there is no other way to say it.

November 2019. Marin County

I arrive on time, as usual, at a high school in Marin. It's good to feel close to home. The fire is under control, but still my nerves are not. Being responsible to my own children, I realize the little details of simply driving across the Golden Gate Bridge could make me vulnerable if there were an earthquake or a fire. I don't want to feel too separated from my children and I realize all these acts we took for granted before have become considerations about safety and responsibility.

Today's class is about social studies and economics. I often learn more than the kids, so I get excited about the day's opportunity.

My schedule is only three classes, well two, with an advisory session. Easy peasy. I get the key, set of instructions, schedules, rosters and head out to the classroom with about ten minutes to spare before the kids arrive. Within that time I must get acquainted with the room, review the sub notes left for me and get ready for the kids. Then I recognize there is no class for two hours. I have two hours to kill! There is no internet so I look around the room.

I'm where I'm supposed to be.

The room is filled with American history books. I poke around. Posters of Gandhi, Thurogood Marshall, Caeser Chavez, Eleanor Roosevelt and Frederick Douglas don the walls. I like the feeling of this room and it tells me a lot about the teacher and his or her point of view, as well as his/her ability to shine a light on the great thinkers, those, at least, I can respect. I plop into the teacher's chair and read about Reagan and Carter. in the text book Why do always feel surprised when I see happy American flags around images of Reagan while the text about Carter is demeaning.

"Carter didn't even have confidence" I read.

There is such a criminal misunderstanding and misrepresentation of Carter's historic *Crisis of Confidence* speech when he was addressing the malaise of the people, not himself. When you look at Reagan's record and his criminal dealings with Iran/Contra and more and he still had a 60% approval rating when he left office and there is a near blackout of anything Carter accomplished either during his presidency or post presidency. How is this all possible?

That "failed" administration of Carter had NOTHING to do with Carter. His leadership will shine because it had EVERYTHING to do with the people, I want to scream. The people became egotistical and squashed Carter and allowed Reagan to not only knock down Carter's energy and environmental programs but ruin us economically with The Reagan Revolution. Why aren't we talking about this?

The Aftershock of Neoliberal Education

If I had my druthers or maybe some guts, I'd storm out of the classroom and march the halls and scream the truths, except they'd fire me and call me crazy. It has been a generation who opted for greed and gave themselves a president to justify that greed. And then decided to ignore that history.

I continue to read. "In the 1980s and 90s greenhouse gasses and global warming were a concern."

"Wow!" Right before our eyes our history is written but we don't connect the dots. Carter tried to steer us away from oil and OPECs stranglehold on our economy!

There is a crass term called "your own fart smells good," and that's pretty much how this last generation can defined itself. I want to say. So I write it down instead.

I have to calm down. My energy is rising and I students are arriving.

Soon I face a group of senior high school students. I take roll and observe how half of the class is made up of immigrant Latinos boys who sit on one side of the room. On the other side are white males. In the middle are the girls. I had never seen such a self induced segregated class in my life. I'm in the hotbed community of Marin County, close to a vast community of Latin American immigrants from Guatemala, Honduras and Mexico, families who are the primary workers of this county who serve as nannies, roofers, housecleaners, day workers. Most of the work is done under the table and helps keep the fanciful homeowners and their large home investments with a median price of $1.4 million dollars in tip top shape without big expenses. An entire generation of wealthy families have been raised by Central Americans, many not being able see their children whom they left in their own homeland in order to come here, make some fast bucks to send back home. Many have not seen their mothers or fathers for up to twenty years because of immigration policies. They are dutiful to their families back in their countries and help support not only their extended families with income, but sometimes their entire communities. Many are building up their retirement back home as that is where their heart resides.

I completely understand their situation given we are the ones who created the trauma, starting long ago but igniting in the 1980s under President Ronald Reagan. There was indigenous genocide of entire communities in the mountains of Guatemala, blood that is still smeared on the palms of our hands in silence today. We supported a war criminal Rios Montt, former president of Guatemala,who was tried and convicted of genocide just a few years ago. Then there were the wars in El Salvador, Nicaragua and Honduras. We supported the oligarchies instead of the people who were fighting for the land, health and education. Maybe today this new generation will have empathy and speak the truth. No, scream the truth. It's time for reconciliation, repatriation and redemption.

I report this as one who has traveled to Guatemala many times, specifically to understand at a deeper level today's disaster. Just this past summer I traveled with a local Guatemalan mother and her two children to her home village where my son and I stayed for several days. My son played with the local children while I stayed in the kitchen to help my friend's mother make tortillas, cheese, tamales and more, recognizing that throughout the day there was a constant stream of neighbors, families and friends stopping by to chat and visit. The food was fresh from the local farms, including the gorgeous purple corn which as made fresh into masa. I couldn't imagine the cost in the US for such food, it being the freshest and purest. And I told the mother, as I reflected on my life living in what is called financially "working poor" conditions in Marin County, sleeping on a sofa and having a minimal social life and hardly seeing my own family members, while stress and anxiety rule my days alone with my computer:

"Heck, your life is richer than my life! You have more daily joy than I do even if you aren't living the jet set, capitalistic American lifestyle that is totally unsustainable!"

The organization 10,000 degrees will deliver a talk about colleges and funding. How fascinating. My film the Man Behind The White Guitar supports this organization! Lua has a fund under her name. I am where I am supposed to be. . . San Rafael High School on Mission Street. The arch Arcangel Rafael seems to be speaking in this hour in order to be redeemed for a gross injustice in history. San Rafael is known as the healer and the messenger, for the angels. We need our angels, our better angels inside and out. I'm getting spiritual. That's how deep this all goes for me!

The speakers of 10,000 Degrees help low income students with college support. They have a multimillion dollar budget and a huge team of employees. My daughter actually got a scholarship from them in 2020 - for a whopping $1000 a year. A year. That was the sum they doled out to everyone. I have begun to believe organizations are nothing less than money institutions when they work this way . . . a rigged system, making themselves look really good but don't deliver the goods. $1000 should be considered pennies today the way they make the students work for that money. The fundraisers bring in a lot of the top dogs, politicians and more. I watch carefully how they work with the students in class.

They ensure every student in the class signs up for FAFSA financial aid for college.

"90% don't succeed with financial aid, so we are here to help," one of the helpers says to me.

I sit back to watch.

Students are handing over the social security numbers in class without parent oversight. What? Is this aiding or abetting debt? The speaker has a checklist, one by one she checks off all the students in the class. What? Many of these kids aren't even headed to college. Isn't there another way? Is a four year college the only way and why do we force it to be the most elite way? The only way? With $7.1 trillion dollars of scholar debt, is it possible this is a wild west land frontier land grab for student money debt? Does the organization get kudos for a record of signing up the most students for FAFSA, a badge of honor that they can boast about at the next fundraiser?

I sit back and think about my early college years. Even though we were broke, my mother had incredible dignity, whether that was right or wrong. I remember asking my mom for help to look for scholarships. "Sweetie, we are white and have a house. Nobody is going to give you money." And instead she took a night job and I took six years to put my self through school with a number of junior colleges, shacking up with a boyfriend to reduce rent and working thirty hours a week to ultimately attend a state college because I had no other choice. My pick had been Santa Barbara UC and I was mad as hell for not going there. But today's perspective leaves me deeply grateful. I finished school debt free. I did it myself and I owed nobody, except my parents, of course. No other institute gets to use my name to create their worth. I'm free. Totally free. And I got a hell of an education at San Francisco State University with true intellectuals, diversity, and community. My fellow students didn't come mostly from elite families but they were down to earth, working class, immigrants and artists. The teachers were stellar.

My recent Master's Degree tells another story.

I owe $15,000 college debt and helped the well manicured lawns of Dominican University look beautiful. The school was forbidden to hold pot luck parties because of the high end union caterers who force them to cater their food, nixing most grassroots, student oriented events. My $20,000 debt helped the caterers, not me. And the gardeners.

What's more? I literally walked into the office and asked for the money to pay tuition and they handed it over to me. As simple as pie, plus years of debt. Was it worth it? I'm still fishing for that answer and I have publicly stated that I would like to return my degree to the school. They have not educated the people, especially with politics. And especially Reagan. That little secret got out when I got canned from the radio program I was hosting at the school, talking politics and Reagan. Was it a coincidence that program got nixed with an email to me just one week before a member of The Vatican came to speak on campus? After all, The Vatican and Ronald Reagan were buddies. And both could be criminally charged for war crimes against humanity, given President Jimmy Carter tried to stop climate change in the late 1970s. The Vatican supported Reagan who knocked down Carter's energy policies that could have saved us all on a planetary level, reducing greatly greenhouse gases. But The Vatican wanted to do business in the former Soviet Union, where they had been forbidden, and they liked Reagan's style.

My disgust about our system continues to grow.

Students are calling their parents for social security numbers without thinking through this carefully. They are asking for private information. I watch in horror.

October 2021, San Francisco County

I'm the P.E. teacher for the day. I put on my hat and try to remember what is the role of a P.E. teacher. I meditate for a few minutes about my own years of physical education back in the day. . . hours of running circles around a field, being forced to do sit ups. I actually don't remember much more than that except those dreary days of having to change clothes with rapid response in a cold locker room that smelled of moist mold and filled with watchful eyes, especially when Aunt Flow came to visit. I was a horridly shy child. Oh, I remember one more incident, biting my finger nails in fear for a week when I had to prove my swim abilities in front of the entire class, and, of course, it came the same week Aunt Flow was visiting. I had never used a tampon before and I was in fear a streak of blood would follow me in the pool with all the boys laughing hysterically at me. I ended up at home with a stomach ache for a few days, a self induced drama that fooled my mother and the school. The fear, ah, the fear. I guess I did prove some good acting abilities.

"Okay, kids, run the field ten laps!"

Oh, I really didn't want to do that. Perhaps I should have had some fun and made them skip, dance or ANYTHING aside from running. But, it didn't matter what I told them. Within minutes some kids literally disappeared. High school students who understood the system, how to duck and cover and find their own way. The other kids gave me the proverbial finger and walked and talked, a perfect opportunity to catch up on gossip, hair styles and Friday night plans.

I sat there wondering what to do. Should I scream at them? Should I mark them down? Report them? But, which kids are they? I was experiencing true mutiny on the big field.

I watch dog walkers onto the field, onto the campus during school hours. What? I learn they are the high end neighbors who apparently can come onto the school field any time they want, using the field like a dog park. Kids are still walking laps. A big fluffy husky comes running up to me freely, unleashed. He heads toward the drinking fountain and licks it (I am horrified), then turns his ass next to the singular tree and takes a full blown chocolate pudding shit. How else do you describe it? I look around for the owner. There is no owner. This dog is as rebellious as the kids! This is disgusting! I want to scream.

Another dog walking neighbor comes around. He has a chip on his shoulder, I see it right away. "Are you the teacher?" He says bluntly to me.

I explain that I'm a sub. He continues to tell me the principal of the school should be demanding the kids to pick up their trash.

"Be a citizen, learn citizenship skills." I watch the husky run away to his far off owner and off they go. The shit is still sitting by the tree attracting flies and is in the path of the returning walking students.

I looked off to the ocean, which I could see from my position. The Pacific Ocean. It gives me calm and big picture perspective.

I truly wanted to tell him and to his other SF Pelosi liberal pieces of shit tp "do it yourself and set an example. Look at what your generation has done to their generation!" But I bite my tongue. It's getting bloody.

Instead I take off my glasses and smile at him. "I guess they learn from us, don't they?" I proceed to tell him about a dog walker in my own neighborhood who picks up plastic and has created art projects. She's constructing animal figures that are going extinct in our generation. I mention the ocean's plastic literally choking life in our oceans.

He grew quiet and I knew I was riding a fine line between getting into trouble by pissing him off with truth or getting through his thick skull. His dog ran off, and so did he. But, the man had a good point, and I knew that. The thick layer of trash on the school yard post the lunch time hour was unacceptable. Layers of potato chip bags, napkins, plastic forks and more.

The bell rang and the kids sauntered off to their classes. As I walked back to the school building and the kids emptied the yard, Alfred Hitchock's movie set was in full operation. That's what it looked like. Seagulls were dive bombing and eating he garbage kids had left behind. What has happened to us? And why do we tolerate this? Why do we allow an educational institution follow a bad pattern when we have all the tools to enable it to be the leader of being resourceful, teaching responsibility to both land and our body and get rid of the proverbial shit that litters our children's world? Where are the teachers? What has happened to our schools?

I went into the girl's locker room for some respite. It was my break time but within minutes it got disrupted by loud clanging. I imagined a mob behind a locked door. What was going on and where are the other teachers? Why am I alone in here? So I drew a breath and carefully opened the door merely to show my credentials.

"I'm only a sub!!!" Use it when it works for you!

"What the fuck. Let us in!" one girl shouted. There were all girls!

"I'm just a sub! I can't let you in until your teacher comes."

"Mother fucker. You are a fucking teacher. That's fucked up," one shouted in my face, with a spray of spit.

On one hand, I liked the girl. She was giving me high status. Yes, I am a teacher. I have authority and a thinking brain! THANK YOU! On the other hand I was worried a fist would come shining toward me on one of this fuck words and knock me out.

I shut the door and locked it. I returned to the field outside more rattled after my break. I felt the gentle ocean breeze on my face before the final class. This is not teaching. This is running an insane asylum.

November 2019, Marin County, CA

I had to indicate a lunch break on my "timesheet." Really? I receive a pitiful wage and I can't leave the campus for the half hour for lunch. They can't pay me a day's wage or cover my half hour? Really?

The Aftershock of Neoliberal Education

My job: I'm to support a young disabled boy. He was pretty self sufficient but needed some assistance during the day. What a testament that our public schools offer support to these children. That's an A plus. And, what a delight! The children were so protective of him. The children augmented any aggressive games to accommodate him. He laughed and he felt a part of it all. I served merely as a silent arm or two arms at times to help him be a fully self sufficient child and get through a normal childhood experience - public school. And the other children got to practice kindness.

My elementary school janitor was highly disabled. When he walked he dragged one of his legs and yet he walked to work every day as he lived just down the street. When mom drove me to school, like other kids, I'd wave to him out the window. He had an entire fan club waiting for him at school. We understand his work was hard on him, but he also had incredible self dignity to work and earn his own way. Everyone respected him. On my final day of school, he wrote special words for me in a book. It took him over thirty minutes to write several sentences, that's how disabled he was. His joints were stiff and his talk was very difficult to understand. When I showed my dad what Mr. Knoll had written, my dad looked at me hard. "You respect what he did for you. That wasn't easy for him." And I did respect it.

But, later much of my glee over that social success story, I got plunged into sadness watching a reading system get implemented. The poor teacher. Another good teacher in a bad system. Who came up with a point system to get kids to read? Who is calling out which books are appropriate? An extrinsic approach to one of the greatest pleasures children could experience by beating it into them.? READ! READ! READ! I mean, why don't we do the opposite approach, given we know how kids operate. NO READING BOOKS, should be written on banners across schools. In no time at all there'd be clandestine societies of children reading the best books.

It could happen. Don't laugh.

Marin County, November 2019

I start the class. An ice breaker.

"Who is President Jimmy Carter? And tell me something about him." I started the class.

"He's dead?" one asked.

"He was a failed president?" Another said.

"Never heard of him." said most.

The Aftershock of Neoliberal Education

I lead a five minute discussion about President Jimmy Carter's energy and environmental policies, given climate change is the hot topic of the times as California burns down. There are more fires, some just up north. Everyone is on alert.

After my talk, a student raised his hand. "So, Reagan is the one who caused climate change?"

I didn't tell him directly except to say, "You are more intelligent than most adults."

I recite my instructions to the class. All learning is on the computer for the hour. Computer learning, thanks to King Bill Gates who has cashed out big. I sit at my desk and watch the students stare at their computers doing whatever work they are required to do. I recall all those crazy studies demonstrating how unhealthy screen time is for our youth and here I sit in a classroom, an institution for learning, and we have had billionaire psychopaths craft our education and we bought it hook, line and sinker. Soon enough there won't be any teachers. Students will log on and follow manufactured learning and they will own our children. Wasn't it Bill Gates who rousted the entire system with his Common Core? Why are we allowing billionaires to control us with all their devices, systems and ideas? Where are our ideas, as the people and educators?

I recall an article from The Federalist, though many publications wrote about it. Common Core had no pilot project before launching. We had a tech billionaire reshape our entire educational model under Obama. I recall that summer when the switch happened, with teachers going bonkers trying to figure out how to reshape how they were teaching. It was a failure. Gates dumbed us down. We were his experiment. We, the people were Gates' experiment when he had no business to muddle with education. Why have we not held him accountable? We need to hold him accountable.

Third period. Not a single student of nearly thirty six graders have ever heard of Carter. I guess it shouldn't be terribly surprising given the school is in one of the wealthiest communities of Marin County. In fact, Habitat for Humanity, Carter's favorite program, got kicked out a number of years ago when they were trying to build a few houses for the needy. This is the heart of neoliberal/Reagan world where the folks cashed out under the trickle down economics of the last forty years and were winners of The Reagan Revolution.

How did I end up in this county? The universe loves to play tricks. And it played a good one on me.

A teachers' union strike has erupted in Sonoma County, just after the fires that have impacted the communities hard. I've been invited to submit my application and make double my rate to $300 day with mileage paid for . . . and more perks, like daily lunch if I'm willing to be a scab. I think about it.

I've never considered being a scab before. But maybe I could use it as opportunity to engage with the students to talk about the most vital political and environmental history that matters to them? I have assuredly tapped into arguably the most powerful propaganda act ever delivered to a nation that is fed straight through our school system. A forty year propaganda narrative that literally made a US President disappear from our consciousness, a president who tried to stop climate change. I think about Reagan who stands as a statue representing our State of California. . . he stands in Washington DC. Nancy Pelosi put him there. How did we miss this?

I have another ugly gut feeling. I'm consolidating my debts, two credit card debts. I've never done this before but given I have at least a job with a day rate nearly the same value as two parking tickets, I figured it was the right time to get my finances in shape. I called a financial consultant or did he call me? It's hard to remember. I started the process with my eyes wide open. I have heard horror stories about people consolidating debt. I didn't need any more surprises in my life.

San Francisco, December 2019

I'm having a momentary breakdown after I walk into a classroom and look at the class assignment. I take two deep breaths and then feel to determined to laugh at the absurdity of what I'm reading and must deliver to an English class of middle schoolers.

My God.

I must pass out articles *The New Play Station* by Microsoft, Sony and Nintendo. It's "Corporate" looking at me straight in the face. On a salary of $150/ay, worth two parking tickets, I am the advertising vehicle for the most profitable corporate enterprises in the world - as an educator.

Am I alone in this world to take witness of these most egregious, in your face, propaganda? What teacher on Earth supports this junk curriculum? It makes you go slowly insane. These are our schools! Our public institutions are not only undermining our children's given right to receive an education to be critical thinkers and learn to stand up to hypocrisy and be a stand for our collective democracy . . . but we are dumbing them down and catering to media entertainment!

I look at the next article. "Sesame Street Birthday" . . . ! It's Big Bird and others celebrating 50 years.

The Aftershock of Neoliberal Education

These children have been designated as "special children." My interaction with them told me something completely different. These are normal children who have been so traumatized by a system that is ill along with teachers who have no business teaching, in this particular case.

I talk to the kids. They are normal. But, they are definitely shut down and made to feel stupid. If you look at kids as being "special" they will become "special," a code word today for not fitting into a system someone believes you have to fit into like a computer chip. We have forgotten what it means to be human.

I could barely function during this hour. I had to plot what to do about this situation, so I took notes. It was all I could do.

The following classes became a blur, but I remember phones in the classroom, students pounding candy. There were narcissistic bullies creating unsafe classrooms, and were not held accountable for their behavior.

That night I attended an evening talk driven by the school district to learn about different pathways to become a teacher. They were trying to address programs for more social justice, more initiatives. They said they wanted more black teachers for the black communities. And I wondered if that is self segregation or is it a smart idea? I feel I'm spinning into a space of knowing nothing. What is right?

Here I have a Master's degree with so many hours in a classroom. I can walk into a classroom as substitute teacher with no training. One merely needs a BA degree and pass a test. But I see in order to be a teacher, you have to spend money. And it's a lot of money. Why isn't there a model to work alongside a teacher, as a mentor while making a living? Imagine the great teachers we could cultivate! I think how much I've already spent on my education with a $20,000 loan to be reimbursed for my Masters in Humanities - now what? The whole system feels rigged. . . to earn a low wage teacher's salary.

Last night San Francisco passed a measure to support housing for teachers. I raise my hand, I don't want special housing! I just want to earn a living wage like a human being! They tried this down in Silicon Valley, last I heard. It's a perfect way to lock people into a system. Why shouldn't teachers make a good solid wage? Why do we do anything possible other than give our teachers what they deserve?

I had one student tell me that if teachers made good money, then people would only do it for the money. He actually believed this. I thought well, hell's bells, we should be giving doctors a pitiful wage! And what about our politicians? Where do people learn such ideas?

I think of my old neighborhood in Fremont. I good solid middle class community where our teachers owned homes next door accountants, lawyers and electricians. It wasn't considered weird. It was normal. Apparently, according to today's standard, we were socialists! We have come to such a brink of insanity that those who haven't lived and experienced a balanced middle class society don't even understand what that means! It also meant, however, that middle class folks, like my family, weren't extravagant. A trip to Hawaii, for example, was extravagant. I knew very few people who got onto airplanes to fly to Europe. If you did, you were elite. The middle class folk went camping, lived simple and didn't even eat out that much. We had community though and knew how to throw a killer Progressive Dinner in our community, where a group of people go house to house for the different courses of a meal and then end up in a hot tub somewhere with kids and parents laughing! That was extravagant for us. And it didn't involve sexual scandals.

I think of Reagan and how Reagan's shadow continues to haunt my life. . .and nobody sees it or wants to talk about it. I think how Nancy Reagan spent $1000 a plate setting for the White House in

1981, an extravagant cost. But, they brought in that extravagance and the rest of the nation followed.

And still no one wants to talk about President Jimmy Carter, a humble president of the US living in a house worth $150,000, the cost of two new automobiles in the county where I live.

Last night I went to a local city council candidate's party post his election in my "liberal" Marin County. Most of the folks have been driving the political scene in Marin for decades. I used to believe the folks were liberal, but over the years I recognized that label no longer defines the "liberal" that I had it defined. The most segregated economic and racial community likely in the country and here are "liberals" running the show, ensuring their big property values stay solid. I hear one old guy complaining about overpopulation and climate change.

I offered, "I know, had we only listened to President Jimmy Carter we wouldn't be in this mess."

His group looked away with discomfort. I chose to dig deeper. "Reagan belongs in a propaganda museum, don't you agree?"

That was the end of that cocktail talk. It was time to leave. And I just couldn't get out of my head that I am living in neoliberal central. I am witness to the greatest illusions in our country.

I write it all down. Maybe one day humor can be ignited through this trauma I've witnessed. At some point, you just have to make yourself a pot of popcorn, sit down and start laughing at what humans are capable of manufacturing! I'll get there one day.

San Francisco, December 2019

I hear the rhythmic repetition by the students. The sound is melodic, beautiful. The students read and record themselves. I introduced myself with a huge smile on my face.

"Wo shi lou shi Babala!" My name is Teacher Barbara.

Memories of my old days of living in China are flowing through my mind as I stand as the substitute teacher in a Mandarin class. And I could feel tears rise in my eyes. What a year it was, filled with fulfilling dreams, learning culture, language and more. Mandarin is a beautiful language!

I had to show the students a film and I watched in delight. At least China respects its teachers! The year I spent teaching at Nanjing University in 1994 and 1995 showed me how respectful Chinese schools are to their teachers and how good the teachers are! I remember well the passion that they hold dear as they support the students. The film was amazing. It portrayed a young Chinese boy who was coming of age and going through the trials and tribulations of becoming a young man, complete with a love affair that hurts him and facing his own feelings of inadequacy. How he pushed his teacher with defiance and how his teacher stood by him, helping him rise to be a better person. Why don't we show our American children such films, those that share the heart of the Chinese people and could inspire us to think differently?

As I rushed out of the house this morning I had grabbed a book that had once been a given to me as a parting gift when I had left for China - *The Art of Teaching*, which was also translated into Chinese. What a coincidence!

Most of the students were Chinese given it's a Mandarin Chinese class which either provided them an easy A or helped connect them to their wondrous history and culture. There were a few white kids and everyone seemed to get along well, from what I could tell. There was one heavy set black girl who came straight to me before the attendance bell rang. She had big brown eyes and introduced herself.

The Aftershock of Neoliberal Education

"I just wanted to give you my name before I get into trouble. My name is Trudy."

I smiled. "You seem wonderful. What possible trouble could you cause?"

"Well. . . she said, "as she looked askance and then bounced off."

I stood there wondering what was in store for me until the bell rang in that moment, my cue to start taking roll.

I started to go down the list, feeling fairly proud that I could pronounce fairly well many of the Chinese names, a little gift of knowledge I received after living and studying in China for a year. As I went down the list one by one I began to witness an incredible act, one that began so slow but picked up incredible speed leaving me almost speechless.

Trudy sat at her desk in front of me and pulled out bags and bags of candy.

"Maybe you should put that away," I say.

Instead, Trudy started giving it out to a lot of the kids so fast and a mob scene grew in front of me so fast. And then someone shouted.

"The lizard! Look Stacy!" Trudy shouted.

I looked at Trudy and she had stood up tall, eyes big and round. Gritted between her teeth, she had a full length of sour tongue candy that was hanging down to her belly. She started chewing really fast. No, not fast. It was akin to a Demonic slurp that moved so fast, as she slurped it into her mouth. I had never seen such an act of slurping in my life, not even noodle slurping in soup restaurants of China where slurping was an act of reverence for the long noodles of life. I witnessed, no doubt, an amazingly talented moment and I had to stop. My eyes nearly turned as big and round. And Trudy continued this slurping, chewing this gum, a two foot specimen, straight into her mouth. The whole class watched, stunned. She performed with a professional finish of licking her fingers and smiling big.

How do you start the class after such a moment? I had to take a moment to collect myself after such a marveled moment. Trudy surely named her act appropriately. "The Lizard."

I was finally able to get through roll and I noticed all the kids were kind to her. I wondered at the incredible diversity in the room and how a cultured language can bring them all together. I watched the children huddle two by two or three by three in the hallways to record on their phones a new language they were learning, quite joyfully. Then I saw Trudy sitting at her desk alone. She was like a lump at the desk. I sat next to her. She refused to pull out her book. She did not want to participate and I wondered why she was in this class. A large black girl with little connection to the Chinese world and who performs lizard acts at roll calling time.

I pulled out a piece of paper. "Trudy, can you write one Chinese character for me?

And she did.

She wrote the number one, a simple Chinese character.

"Okay, how about a second character?" I asked her.

She did and she wrote quickly all the numbers up to 10. I was pretty impressed.

"Trudy, can you write your name in Chinese?"

She did and it was amazing. Mind blowing amazing.

Trudy would not write anymore and then she started to cause some problems by distracting other children and wandering into the hall, creating fear in me that she might wonder off. She was a wild card. And she was beginning to take all my energy as I worked to protect the other children from her distractions. How can that be acceptable in a classroom, when one person creates so much work for a single teacher, stealing that time from the other students who are doing their work and want to learn? It's impossible and it's a system set up to fail.

In that moment the vice principal came around to check in. I liked him a lot. He was doing his best and surely was marveling, like me, how crazy the system had become.

I explained that Trudy was becoming distracting but I also showed him Trudy's writing. She was gifted, highly gifted. And clearly this social structure was not working for her, as it doesn't for many kids. It's loud, crowded and too distracting for those who are sensitive. There have been times I've seen children with their hands over their ears due to the loudness that many people have grown to accept. You can't think in these environments which have become little more than social pressure pots ready to pop. And for those children who might have more challenges in life, they do their best to be recognized even it means creating distractions. I liked Trudy a lot. And I wanted to be there for her but do I ignore all the other students for one?

As I monitored Trudy the other children began to change their behavior. I started catching more and more on video games or on the phone with their friends instead of doing their work.

So I brought them all back into the class room for the last few minutes to hold them with a story. I shared with them my stories about China twenty years ago and what it was like to be a waiguaren (a foreigner) there. I told them how difficult it was for me to learn the language and how lucky there were to study this ancient language.

I was pretty exhausted at the end of the day. I didn't leave right away. I sat alone at the desk listening to the children run out of the halls. I quietly and reflectively wrote my notes for the teacher who I could see cared deeply for the students.

The school janitor entered the room, the same one from the days before. We chat. He's black and grew up in the ghetto "where there was violence and drugs" he made sure to tell me. But he stayed straight and is the proud father of three. One just graduated from college, another is an artist. The janitor showed me the artwork of his son and it is truly amazing work. As a single father, he lives in Vacaville, which is a three hour commute for him each way, to keep this job. He couldn't afford San Francisco anymore. I can tell he's a really smart guy and "fights" by staying true and honest. I could see him on a stage. "The Janitor Talk" where he gets real. How is it that the janitor feels more human to me than so many others I know who have fancy titles, prestige and money?

"My boys won't ever have to do this," he says.

I say, "Sir, there in no shame in making an honest living. You've got more than most billionaires at this stage."

And I meant it.

December 2019

I have spent five months looking for a roommate. People would book an appointment. I'd spend an entire weekend cleaning and preparing the apartment. Then, they wouldn't show up. They wouldn't call or send a message to cancel and I'd sit there in my clean apartment marveling at the fact that our society is losing the basic elements that keep a civil society together, a social contract that communicates and treats each other with human dignity and respect. How has it gotten this bad?

I'm now in an economic crisis. I don't tell my kids how close I am to losing this apartment. Recently I got a note about consolidating my debt. So, that's my plan. After lengthy conversations with a financial rep from a company, I am told to meet the notary to sign the documents. They will meet me anywhere which I deem as a kind, supportive act. I suggest the local cafe at 7pm at night. I think I can consolidate and bring down my monthly bills and get on track after facing credit card and university debt that is crushing me each month. I have a roommate moving in next week, which will put me in the corner of the living room with a partition for privacy. I'll change my clothes in the shared bathroom. I am still going to the local foodbank. minimizing everything possible. Still, I'm barely making it financially. Is there any end in sight?

It was dark at night and I sat in the cafe where I was to finalize the low interest loan, to help me out of debt. She came in . The notary. Until that moment I had been reflecting on what the financial consultant had said to me at the end of our conversation,

"It'd be a good idea to close your bank account if your credit card is with them, especially if it's a credit union."

"Why is that", I had asked.

"Credit unions work with different laws than banks."

"This is all legal, right? The loan?"

He paused. "Yes.

"They are a community bank. I don't want to leave them." I say. I liked my bank, which is a weird statement to say these days.

"I just wanted to warn you", he says. "Also, there is no pressure to use our attorneys."

"What does that mean? Why would anyone come after me? I'm just trying to pay rent and feed my family. Honestly. Why would I need lawyers?" I reply.

I continue to reflect on this conversation and my stomach begins to shift, as if telling me something. The notary enters, and I see her fancy diamonds on her fingers. I get a strange feeling that this is wrong, but I have no real reason to believe that yet. I decide to be careful. She hands me the document which they had refused to show me before. Why was that? Isn't it better to review a financial document before meeting with the pressure to sign?

I begin to read the document. And I see how wrong it is. A set up! A set up to lure me with money to pay off my debts but with the most crushing consequences including lawyers fees and more. I imagine what would happen if I lost my job. I'd be stuck in a system with this company for the rest of my life!

There is pressure to sign. She's texting the financial consultant. I don't like pressure.

I push the document toward her. "This language is a deal breaker for me." I say solidly and sternly.

She pauses. She sees that I see through the charade. And she bites her lip. She knows I'm looking at her as the con artist.

"I suppose we women ought to stick together better, shouldn't we?"

"Yes, we should." I answer. "I'll pay you for you time. I know they probably won't pay you as a notary," I offered.

"No, you don't need to pay me."

She walked off into the dark night as I sat finishing my tea. I won that battle. I was almost conned, exploited. And it opened me up to fight I must prepare for. The fight would come, and I wasn't even sure exactly what is was. But I could feel it.

November 2019, Marin County

Each of the children have IPads. I've been told over and over again that this is a sign of a school one should be proud of. An IPad is the symbol of that success. The school is helping the children prepare for their future. I can't shake the thoughts of the costs of all these IPADS, bought for outrageous amounts of money by our tax dollars, that there is a high tech executive laughing his head off as he jets off to Hawaii and puts his own children into private Waldorf Schools that haven't sold out their souls.

I enter the science classroom. A youngish teacher is behind a podium getting ready for the day. The classroom is empty of any sign of student life. Cabinets are closed and walls are bare. I see no paper, pens or other messy classroom signs that would suggest there is any learning in this classroom except for one counter filled with gooey and colorful models of blocks. And I see one student. He's my favorite. Likely the most challenging student at the school who has a bad wrap but is sticking like glue to his creative mind against all odds.

He's working before class hours on his project. Adding glue, making a mess but doing it.

"Save some of that glue for other students, Ian. This isn't your period" the teacher says across the empty classroom to Ian.

It sounded like an admonishment to me so I decide to step in and soften the atmosphere. I wondered why this teacher wouldn't encourage Ian by acknowledging he was here on his own terms to work on his project!

The Aftershock of Neoliberal Education

The student stayed diligent with his work but I could feel him shift a bit, like carrying a weight on his shoulders.

"Ian, that is really amazing what you've created. Can you tell me about it?"

He started to explain the structure but the bell rang and he left, walking the halls alone. I had never seen him with another child cheerfully, something I would love to see. One of the teachers later told me that he comes from a poor family and his older brother is a trouble maker. It's likely he's going to be trouble too.

I thought such teachers should be fired from their jobs with that sort of attitude. When you lose hope in a student, it's time to retire. Never lose hope in a student. It's a middle school kid, for God's sake!

The class was about to begin and I was given my instructions. Today's class is about nutrition. The students will do the work on the computer. I just need to roam around and make sure they are all on task.

*Don't grade down for spelling mistakes. Let student use her spell check.

*Allow the calculator or multiplication chart on tests.

*Google classroom, Google Earth, Google Daily Nutrition are the tools used.

I roam around. I squat next to students and ask them about the work they are doing, filling in bubbles, giving information about nutritional values of the food they had eaten before.

I ask a student. "Do you remember any of this information?"

"Nope."

Even the kids in middle school are smart enough to know this is a charade.

As I watched each kid hold a computer, I was reminded who was making the bucks. Education is now a money game, a high tech takeover of our children where everything is documented, filed and saved. I wondered about little Ian and getting a bad rap during middle school. Could that bad rap follow him into adulthood? What about elementary school? Everything is being documented about our children! EVERYTHING! And it's owned by big tech who are cashing out with our tax dollars to do nothing short of surveillance of our children on every level.

Our schools are leading this effort. This is not education. This is tactical power to own our children.

November, 2019

It's my son's birthday. His father makes the call of how to celebrate his birthday. In my next life I'm getting sperm donor.

His father wants to take my twelve year old son to a paint ball facility where children don military clothing and carry faux militarized guns and pretend they are killing each other. And this is joyful and fun.

Instead of protesting, which I should have done with picket signs outside his house, I decide to join them and pay witness to what our society is doing to young boys. And I watch with absolute horror. How can we sanction this type of entertainment for our children, a violent form of play that conditions them to believe that carrying guns, shooting each other and laughing about it, while other full grown men join the game, is healthy for a society?

This was NOT how I had wanted to raise my son but I have no say. I remember sailing on the sea with my young sweet boy riding on the bow, a feeling of freedom with the water splashing underneath and the big blue sky above. People working together raising sails and feeling the hearts of the wind and water connect around you - a feeling of beauty, bliss and freedom. And, now I sit in this hell hole of male toxicity. It was his father's encouragement. What happened to my ex-husband the man I used to know?

It's the same as our society. Do men not see how stupid they look playing war games? Full grown men with our boys indoctrinating our beautiful boys.

I had interviewed Brian S. Wilson once, a Vietnam Veteran who today at age 81 lives in Nicaragua. He lost both his legs after throwing himself in front of a train in Northern California that was headed to Central America during the 1980s to deliver arms for their civil war. We supported the bad guys, the oligarchy, history that still has yet to be reconciled. He told me in the interview that his anger to this day is how he was used as a privileged white boy to learn to hate others and believe that being a soldier was justified. He was used and abused to help the elite warmongers, those cashing out in a system that is so unjust. And when he recognized how he had been used, he went on a hunger strike and has dedicated his life to peace. To this day he has not been recognized by our political leaders and likely not in any of our history books, at least that I know of. He is a true American hero.

We have a school crisis. Kids are shooting up other kids in our schools across the country. We call them psychotic. No, our culture has become pyschotic.

November 2019

Full moon last night. There's a teacher's strike in Sonoma and the money they'd pay me is double my day rate. Do I do it? Free lunch. Free breakfast. Mileage paid for. They'd treat me better as a scab than as a teacher. I'm still mulling it over.

I fill out the paperwork and the strike happens when I'm already committed to work in San Francisco. No, I wouldn't have done it anyway . . . but I understand the utter lure, especially for those of us who are hungry.

I had my entry planned out. I like to fantasize. I'd walk through the strike line with my own banner.

"Where were you in 1981! Feel it!" It's my anger speaking. Where is Jimmy? That's my social justice speaking.

It could have been possible that I'd do a turn and join them for the strike and square in the face "F you" to the school administrators. Give respect to your teachers!

That's in my blood and there is no organization to support and have the backs of subs. I'd be out of a job in no time as they all went back to work with pay raises and I'd be sitting alone on my arse.

I spent the weekend with my ex and watched the film *Mr. Fantastic*, which tells you everything you might know. A powerful film which gives the illusion that patriarchy, authoritarianism is the justified. I see the mother character, who never appears in the film, minus two sex scenes, urging the man on with her loving look. She died by suicide after depression, and bouts of the so called mental illness. I look at her husband in the film who is being framed as the amazing father and then I get why she probably went crazy. And for some weird reason the father is heralded at the end. That's why too many of us are going crazy.

The son in the film disappointingly submits to the father's will and forgoes university, an effort he made behind his father's back with his mother's help. The father goes irate, feeling betrayed by his son instead of feeling proud that his son made an independent effort and succeeded. In the end, the son foregoes the university and does what his father wants him to do. . . justifying in my mind's eye that the son became the follower of his father's wishes instead of following his own heart. And that was celebrated at the end of the film and by my ex husband as we squabbled over the values. I suppose that is why he is my ex husband. And I see I will have a journey with my own son who I wish will follow his heart and what HE wants to do instead of the demands either of us put on him. Those were the values I was raised with and I stand by them.

The spirit of the father in the film is exactly the problem we are facing today. I think of the film and about the mother. The idea of "do as I say "as a formula for being a good student, which in my mind's eye is nothing short of teaching authoritarianism, instead of nurturing a person's desires and allowing their own gifts and freedom to shine.

November 2019 - Evening Teacher's Conference, San Francisco

I attend an evening conference to learn how to become a paid, certified teacher in our public school system. I have nearly $20,000 in debt for my Master's Degree which means diddly squat in our public schooling institutions except for junior colleges where I would be allowed to teach. But, for any schooling under that? Nada. So, I go to the conference to see if there is a way I can pay rent, parent my kids, get paid, go to school and get certified to be a teacher in our public schools earning diddly squat.

There was a fairly large collection of people, many of whom were substitute teachers. There was some free fruit and crackers on a table and I felt I scored for dinner. That is the level I have reached, I thought. It's like being a 21 year old back in the good old college days when I was broke and hungry. Not much has changed in over 30 years, except for one thing. It's all gotten far worse.

"We want people, teachers, who our students can identify with, in our neighborhood. Connection. We need more people of color," the speaker said.

I looked at my white hands. It's funny, I was told earlier during our substitute seminar to head out to those very neighborhoods in order to foster diversity and connection. When does such a narrative, as shared by the speaker, become a wonder of self segregation? I'm trying not to place too much judgment on the color of skin but shouldn't we focus on good teachers, diversity and tolerance? What is right?

I learn about the different paths of becoming a teacher. There is not a single path that is financially viable for me to pursue without going further into debt. I think of the Waldorf Schools where teacher training is conducive to those who truly want to teach and earn a living. It's a brilliant system of working as assistants and being paid a fair wage during the week and using your weekends twice a month to pursue your learning. The public school system is set up to fail. It's alienating so many good teachers. Where is the wisdom?

I walk out into the dark night with grapes in my hand. At least I got dinner.

November 2019, San Francisco

Up at 5:30 am, out by 6am. It's dark and I had 5 minutes to grab coffee at the shop for the 30 minute drive to SF, no traffic.

Yesterday as I ushered twenty five kids from the play yard to the classroom, an act that takes up a good chunk of energy, keeping twenty five jumping beans together without falling apart, making noise or causing mayhem. I was reminded of my cattle driving experience when by horse, I had to push a head of 100 long horn cattle across the mountain for the winter pasture. It was the greatest lesson in my life. If you go too fast, they scatter. If you go too slow, they stop and graze and won't move unless you give them a hard holler.

Getting them to move again takes even greater determination because they have discovered their own will and power, how to be stubborn and hold their ground, while eating the luscious grasses.

These are my thoughts as the kids ascend two flights of concreted steps to the second floor of our classroom. I'm taking up the rear with four boys who have discovered how to graze. I want to give them my cowgirl scream but that would get me fired.

We're near the top of the stairs when suddenly a girl in front of me collapses onto me. Her full body weight, like lead, falls right into my arms. Fortunately I had my sure footing, completely by chance. And I had my Mama Bear reaction that was groomed by my own children. I caught her without tumbling down the stairs myself. She would have tumbled had I not been there. I looked behind me. It was a long way down. I had been warned a student in class had been getting seizures that last 15-20 seconds. Clearly she was the student.

I laid her down safely on the landing while a group of kids circled us. I had to monitor her while telling the jumping beans to jump into the classroom quietly and wait for me. Yeah, right.

Once the student snapped back and woke up, she started to cry. I had a single child who needed attention and needed to descend the steps to the wellness center. Could I trust a student or do I leave an entire room of kids by themselves? That is a risk. Both scenarios are a risk! I could have problems with either choice! How do teachers manage this volume of children with no support?

Our system is not set up for this. One human being in charge of the health, emotional health, social health and academic health of 25-35 jumping beans or cattle . . . or children . . . for $150 a day which will not even cover rent in a shared two bedroom apartment!

I think back to my father and those 11,500 families who stood up to a president willing to lose everything for honesty and fair wages. The Hero of the Republican Party, one who was inducted into the Labor Hall of Fame just last year, as I stand in a school named after Senator Diane Feinstein in a district represented by Congresswoman Nancy Pelosi . . . and I stand even taller.

"Fuck this shit". My mantra. It's wrong. The system is wrong.

I finally entrust two students to walk carefully down the stairs with the young girl as I walk into a chaotic classroom of young children taking advantage of the fact that no teacher is monitoring them. I am the sub, so I take position.

"Okay, kids. I'm the leadership coach and I'm looking for leaders. You'll get the star by your name for your teacher."

The classroom quiets down. And I feel my power.

November 2019, San Francisco

I sit in the car at 6:45am taking a deep breath, gaining my composure before my day's assignment. I think how the Republican Party "Hero" stands in

Washington DC representing the State of California. Ronald Reagan, the kingpin of neoliberal policies!

How did that happen? And who was there before him? So, I pull out my computer and Google it. A man's name appears. Starr King. Who the hell was Starr King?

I read.

Starr King was a guy who got California involved to help the Civil War cause. He was a preacher.

I read more . . . he was highly respected. He even has a mountain named after him in Yosemite and stood tall for California in Washington DC representing our state for eight decades. But there isn't much more information about him. I had never heard of him before.

But, I start laughing out loud. It's how the universe works. Starr King. . .something big is getting ready to shine. I can feel it. You can hear it in his name.

I head to the classroom and the teacher is there. I like him immediately and can tell everyone does. He knows his job well, he respects the children and he makes the feeling in the classroom rich and joyful. He gets me busy with the kids doing simple worksheets for the morning hours.

The Aftershock of Neoliberal Education

"They know what to do," he says.

I see awards behind his desk and I hear how the children talk to him and how he talks to the children. There's kindness with firmness. I listen and watch. I want to learn.

When the class comes in after lunch. I follow his instructions carefully.

"Turn on the music," one of the children tells me. And that's exactly what the teacher's instructions tell me what to do.

So I do. It's cue'd up and the music starts to play "Thank you for the music" by ABBA. The children start singing too, full tilt. And it's hard not to join in!

The smiles are infectious. The children are happy and joyful. When was the last time I saw such a joyful class like this?

"Thank you for the music, the songs I'm singing
Thanks for all the joy they're bringing
Who can live without it, I ask in all honesty
What would life be?
Without a song or a dance what are we?"

I read "Caterpillar Going To The Garden"

I take them outside to play and I look to the grey sky with the American flag and the California Bear. There's a star too. Maybe it's the spirit of California waving to me. The Mama Bear. Magic. I feel this. I feel freedom coming. Why do I keep thinking these things? And what freedom is that I feel is coming?

There's quiet time. I read the quotes posted on the classroom walls along with awards, images and other inspirational messages.

"The happiest people don't have the best of everything. They just make the best of everything."

A RAVE Distinguished Award for excellent teaching.

The Greatest Scientists are artists as well."

"Imagination circles the world."

"Stuffing info into children as fast as possible is as nourishing as wolfing down a Big Mac."

"Instruction time for play helps younger children develop their social and language skills, their creative powers and their ability to learn."

There is nothing like walking out of a school refreshed that a single human being, a teacher, is bringing so much happiness and nourishment to our children, the people of the next generation. And this teacher just gave me hope, like Starr King . . . a light to shine our path.

Our teachers need salaries like the highest paid doctors. If we actually invested in good education that is nourishing and balanced, it could essentially up end the entire medical system of mental health and dietary issues, inciting a health revolution. Why do we validate this idea of paying doctors and therapists such high salaries and our teachers criminally low wages when we could solve so many of our problems from the get go? I would put this teacher front and center of that revolution and we'd all be singing . . . no . . . screaming. . .

"Thank you for the music, the songs I'm singing
Thanks for all the joy they're bringing
Who can live without it, I ask in all honesty
What would life be?
Without a song or a dance what are we?"

November 2019, Marin County

Impeachment Hearings started today. Too many of our leaders didn't graduate from kindergarten.

I woke up at 4am and wrote to Nancy Pelosi asking her to remove the Neoliberal President Ronald

Reagan out of Washington DC and return Starr King to the platform. I cc'd Noam Chomsky, LA Times and Jimmy Carter. I don't expect to hear anything back. Though once I did hear from Noam Chomsky who validated my position on Ronald Reagan. Nancy Pelosi's office kicked me out and threatened me with arrest for standing in her office screaming at the top of my lungs to help support my Jimmy Carter initiative, the California State Legislative Resolution to honor Carter. My screaming was more about my intention to hold Nancy Pelosi in esteem, hoping desperately she would support it so she would not fall into the utter pool of demise of the neoliberal mud. I was screaming for her benefit, truly. I had hoped for one bit of evidence to show she would not completely fall when we do begin to recognize these last 40 years of The Reagan Neoliberal Era and those who brought on these policy horrors that have ruined us. But, no chance. There will come a day when I'll scream "Biden, Take Down That Statue!" and Pelosi and her Queendom will also fall. I do my best to have others' backs but not when they step into the mud themselves and choose not to listen.

I sit in my car now in the city of Tiburon "the shark." appropriately named given it is a neoliberal hotspot with extreme wealth, those who have cashed out these last 40 years. I will sub for a music teacher today, middle schoolers, the same age as I was when

The Aftershock of Neoliberal Education

my father stood for honesty against the neoliberal Reagan and the federal government in 1981.

As I left my dark apartment, before the sun rose, I spotted on my coffee table a necklace, that of a black star. I think of David Bowie and his Black Star album and his message to us about living before the mystery takes us away. I think of that sea star of Santa Barbara UC, the one I saw as a near 13 year child sitting in a plastic bin, alone, prepared for the science department. It spoke to me, I swear it did. It told me it didn't belong in a plastic bin and it should be returned to the ocean. . . or maybe to the sky. Or, did I dream that?

I get ready to enter the school Del Mar, of the sea. Life is poetry in the making for me, connections of spirit. Life is poetry for us all, if we choose to stop and listen.

Greta Thurnburg begins her voyage back to Spain. I prepare for my new voyage toward freedom. I must believe I'm on this voyage being guided by a star, a dark star. I feel it in my bones, as crazy as that might seem to those who have lost their own spiritual meaning in this neoliberal world that has cast a shadow on all our good values.

Of course, my first class had to be math. I decide to be the good leadership model for the day to step up into the dark unknown, conquer my own fears and show the kids to be fearless in life, as I face head on math equations that I want to run from. Math that has concrete answers, or so we think. And no Bill Gates or any other big tech STEM propagandists who wants workers for cheap will EVER get me to like math or even want it in my life. I mean, how is it possible that we have calculators, computers and all the devices created to "make our lives easier" and it's all come out the opposite? Our lives are frenetic, insane rat wheels as we all go slowly broke and crazy. Technology lied and we should imagine ourselves in that first Apple commercial running slow motion through a crowd with a fat sledgehammer prepared to shatter the big screens. It's a pure example of what you put out comes right back to you. I must believe that Apple Founder Steve Jobs is rolling in his grave. Did he really believe tech domination in our lives would become so invasive and controlling?

My next class is a guitar class. How did that happen?

I unlock the door to the room for a group of kids my age when my father stood in 1981. I felt like I was staring at my childhood. The strike that killed my guitar lessons and here I sit in a class with children my age as they play the guitar?

It was a beautiful room. Seven students sat in front of me with their guitars. Jazz posters were hanging on the walls, along with other posters of all the classical masters next to a big map of the world. The memories were spinning through my mind of sitting so quietly in my guitar teacher's studio, listening to him play so pleasantly and having the eyes of the masters watch us. There we were in the city of Fremont, the land of the Ohlone, the end of the BART line and a suburban city once filled with meadows, oaks and creeks being taken over by fast food restaurants, shopping malls, bowling alleys and gas stations.

I pretended I knew more than I did. I held the guitar and I smiled. I made a film about a guitarist. I tell them my story twirling my sea star around my neck and losing my lessons in the great 1981 National Strike. It's history, after all.

I pick up one of the guitars and play Greensleeves, the song that was presumably commission by King Henry VIII for his girlfriend Catherine of Catherine of Aragon after he dumped his wife, banishing her from ever seeing her own daughter again. Of course, King Henry then went on a head chopping spree of his later wives and we still have his portraits hanging in museums intact. Such tells us everything we need to know about Western Society. He should be hung by his genitals. Maybe there's still hope.

The kids begin to play "Señorita" Shawn Mendes and Camila Cabello. I feel my body move as this incredibly talented youthful group create this music bouncing off the walls of the classroom, all engrossed in their instruments. I watch their fingers and how they look at each other as the rhythm builds, smiling. I keep from standing up and dancing but I can feel my body move and an energy inside heal me from the inside out, remembering that young child in me who had no inhibitions or fears and just wanted to be free and dance. I feel it in me about to release, but not here and not now. I'm remembering those nights dancing at the local club Star Gaze, moving bodies until 2am, feeling like the rebels when all we young people wanted to do was to laugh, dance and be happy. Why were we made to feel like rebels enjoying such simplicity? The music makes you feel love again and to scream to the world to love each other and dance! Maybe that is sure rebellion today.

I love it when you call me señorita
I wish I could pretend I didn't need ya
But every touch is ooh-la-la-la
It's true, la-la-la
Ooh, I should be runnin'
Ooh, you know I love it when you call me señorita

I lock the door with one more glance of the instruments strewn across the room. It's like having the key to the secret of hope for us all. . . to unlock that music that's in all of us, to feel what these youth just felt and what they had just given me. It's a release to see that I am still a child, as youthful as ever, and I've been educated for too long to play an adult role when there is no such thing. We are all children just wanting to play, laugh and dance, aren't we? What's stopping us?

I lock the door with a promise that one day I'll unlock that proverbial door. And I renew my vow. I am not a substitute teacher. I am a leadership coach. My name is Barbara McVeigh and being a substitute teacher is my super power.

Move over Greta.

December 2019, San Francisco

I do my duty - I wake up at the crack of dawn, fill up the gas tank, eat a piece of bread with peanut butter for breakfast as I cross the bridge to San Francisco for another day of subbing. I'm happy to have this job. I need money. I need to pay the rent. I need to feed my children. And I am having one wild time doing this work, getting deep into where our public schools are today and connecting to the youth people who feel locked up in a system that just no longer makes sense. I have no idea what my assignment will be today. I've learned to be flexible, have confidence and get through the day without screaming, turning into the spinning head exorcist child or throwing a tantum. I'm groomed, civilized, smooth with a smile on my face. These kids have trained me from being raw and messy to being refined and cooked. Or so I tell myself until the end of the day. And this was one of those days.

"They are special needs children," I'm told at the office as I collect the classroom key and roster. I walk into empty classroom which looks set for a kindergarten class. One area is roped off with big stuffed animals. There are desks and chairs. The loud bell rings and the children come. I'm still smiling until I reposition to see the challenge before me.

The middle school children had extreme disabilities. Most were even unable to acknowledge me in front of the classroom much less follow any classroom instructions. They would burst out screaming, one was trying to grab my clothing as I walked by, while another sat in a wheelchair half asleep. TAnother couldn't have paper at his desk as he would immediately tear it up and stuff the shredded strips into his mouth and chew worrying me that he would choke. He needed an aid next to him constantly monitoring his hand movement.

But it was another child who alarmed me the most. He began to bang his head on the desk, again and again and again. This was NOT a classroom. Every single child needed full attention just to stay alive for that one hour or more. And while I was busy trying to give some semblance of instructions to simply color a picture of forest animals and desert habitat, a nature lesson, I didn't realize there was a whole other group behind the partition where the stuffed animals were residing.

I walked over when I had a moment to see more young bodies simply laying limp on the floor. One was in diapers. All aides were on their phones, texting and watching videos. One aide even had the audacity to share a book he was reading about racial justice. Yes, it was a good book but he had a job to do and that was taking care of this middle school highly needy youth. He was hardly an adult himself, likely getting paid piss wages.

And therein lies the problem. The more vulnerable or needy you are, the more exploited you get. A school system sets it up for young people with little experience to take charge of those who won't complain. Who else would take the job?

The room was disgusting and I wondered what would it look like if seriously trained alternative teachers were to enter this room with art therapy, music, dance and other elements to help these young people. Treating them like five year olds is not the answer. It's a waste of money, time and energy and it's likely creating more trauma for these highly disabled people.

I think of a center in Marin County called Cedars which supports a community of those with development disabilities since 2019. With weaving and other amazing arts, transforming lives into productive, meaningful lives instead of a holding tank to take government tax payer money and bring in boxed schooling with ideas of keeping up with a system.

Why do we choose not to think out of the box? Why have we succumbed to such a diseased culture of exploitation?

December 2019, Private School, Marin County

My little classroom is behind a stage in the music room, a school that sits on a hill and serves some one of the most elite communities of Marin. I watch the cars drive up - Volvo, BMWs, SUVs, and I think about Jesus Christ and his messages and how is it possible we believe that big money is somehow sanctioned by a religious belief.

I think of my Celtic roots as I walk into this Catholic School. My pre Christian heritage. Those roots have been growing inside of me these last years, a return to my ancestral spirit. Even if there are few written records about that time, one can still feel it, if one stops to feel.

The Aftershock of Neoliberal Education

But I see the community that this school shares and that is impressive and inspiring. News comes about someone's death in the family. In a heartbeat, the classrooms convene in the church and sing. The children are recording a song for the person in need, a message for hope and love. I nearly tear up seeing such a support network with clearly a staff that cares deeply for the children and for the community.

There is happiness and joy. The school is small and inside it's not necessarily fancy, as it might appear on the outside. But there in an intention to be supportive, respectful and kind, of course, for a high tuition price.

Why is that?

I help a second grade teacher prepare projects for Christmas. As she doles out Santa Clause projects and they sing religious songs, I immediately feel uneasy recognizing that in public schools these cultural acts would not be allowed and deemed inappropriate. It's been such a long time since I've talked to children openly and joyfully about Santa coming down the chimney or baby Jesus in a manger. And though I am not Christian, I see a spirit of goodness emanating and I'm at peace with that.

And as I think about my Celtic heritage, one that was nearly eliminated from planet Earth long ago, it's a spirit that still remains and maybe we all can just rejoice in what each other has and know that it was a long time ago. And now we have a future to build, one that we want that includes diversity and raising the spirits of long ago.

Besides, I like singing Santa songs.

January 2020, Marin County

I'm relieved that I don't have to cross the Golden Gate Bridge and make the long drive into The City. Today I'm assigned to a local school known for its high Latin American immigrant community, a community I appreciate and enjoy. I'll be able to speak a little Spanish and be with children who come from a highly sophisticated cultural heritage although our capitalistic ideas tend to shame them into the ever popular slogan that "they are poor," which indirectly means that they are desperate, likely uneducated and come from families who need leadership. I've always thought this concept was upside down and backwards, because I have always learned from the Latin American communities about culture, respect, community and family, the bonds that keep people together and happy.

I'm a roaming sub for the day. Class to class I go each hour to fill in for a different teacher. Nobody really knows me but the keys around my neck indicate I'm an official, not just a lowly sub. So I walk that walk. For all they know, I'm the head honcho from the main district office. Or, better yet, I'm a superior sub, who has been trained to turn on a dime, take over any class from kindergarten to 12th grade with gifted children, those with disabilities, second language learners, angry or happy students and classrooms lacking a lick of instruction. I'm a professional substitute teacher, a leadership coach, bad ass, ready to take on the whole educational institutions in our country to show what a farce it is! So I walk that way! I change my gait. I carry my packet of emergency procedures and class schedule around like I'm somebody people will notice and should either run in fear from, if they feel guilty, or get behind to revolutionize our public schools.

The kids even look at me. I got this.

I enter a classroom validating that I was right! A full class, mostly of fifth grade Guatemalan children. Most speak English and are a complete delight to me with their happy smiles and cheerful greetings. They show respect minus a few wiggly boys. They are not malicious just energetic, a quality that would likely get them into trouble at school with a label that they are malicious. I've seen it before.

I look at the teacher's notes, and I realize I'm in for a challenge. My stomach tumbles into disgust as if I just ate a plate of spoiled beans. I have to use the upcoming Superbowl as the foundation of lessons for the day. The American Superbowl! I have definitely stepped into the devil's cave. That's how I feel. The American Superbowl Football Game? As a learning tool?

A little bit about me . . . I loathe American football. In my humble view, we have allowed a highly male toxic game that uses violence and boys in tight pants to throw a ball back and forth on a groomed field into some sort of mark of societal greatness. Add skimpy dressed pretty girls on the sidelines cheering the boys on while spectators eat the most disgusting food possible and there you have it - what has become a symbol of American culture.

Few people know that such games were used by the English royalty to groom citizens for war. It's a perfect mentality to create if you want to rule . . . that there is a winning side and a losing side. The more you grunt and tackle, the better you are and the more cheers you get. You become a hero. American football mentality represents to me everything that I find disgusting about our culture and what it's become. Violence, driven by competition and the need for boys to feel macho by holding a ball and running back and forth.

I raise my hand. I feel we could do far better.

The Aftershock of Neoliberal Education

The upcoming game is between the San Francisco 49ers, a name that derived from the gold panning exploitation of California in the 1849s, those trying to get rich by raping the land, displacing and slaughtering Indigenous people while California gold sits in vaults in The Vatican of Rome today. They play against The Kansas City Chiefs. And you know where I could go with that one.

I'm not just disgusted. I'm embarrassed to look at these youth. Many of them come from Indigenous roots of Mayan Temples, forests with jaquars and Quetzales, a national bird with a prophesy that claims that when the bird sings, the Mayan and others will be free. The Mayan festivals honor family. Art and music are so far beyond most American pop tunes today, including those sung and danced on The Superbowl field.

How do I do this? I feel like one of those early indoctrinating villains during colonizing times. What do I do?

I had just read the previous day about the hypocrisy of The Kansas City Chiefs dressing up like American Indians. The sport creates concussions, brain injuries, violence, drunken behavior, egos. Sorry if I offend anyone, but I'd much rather have the wind in my hair or dance the tango. And those Tango and Salsa guys are far more sexy, which I tell the students.

I'm joking.

I highlight in the reading that I must give that the food consumed on this day of American national celebration at the greatest volume, aside from Thanksgiving. Yes, hot dogs and corn dogs! I look at these Latino kids who come from a food culture, knowing the sound of wind in the corn fields, what it means to pull a potato from the earth or make tamales in an adobe or other traditional home in Guatemala using a stone, food that is divine and sacred. And here in America I have to talk about factory slaughtered animals that are ground up and stuffed into hamburgers and hotdogs as if they represent some great society.

I think about the two statues standing in Washington DC. Juniper Serra, a colonizing Catholic who disrupted the Indigenous people and President Ronald Reagan whose capitalistic policies have ruined us all this past generation, including Guatemala, when he supported genocide against the Mayan Indigenous in the 1980s.

Congressman Jared Huffman had said it to me once. "We can do much better."

Yes, we can.

January 2020, Marin County

I look across the room and eye the Beatles walking across the crosswalk, crossing the street. Here I am in a county famed for its music culture, reveling in The Grateful Phil Lesh restaurant of Terrapin Crossroads where you can, in person, witness that generation who has cashed out under neoliberalism with fanciful, expensive dinners on the waterfront. I remember my first Dead Concert, sitting on the earthy ground and watching everyone get high around me. The generation stayed true to its roots . . . it got high on money, feeling good.

That's where my literary mind goes sitting in a math and science class. I look at the 8th grade textbook sitting at the teacher's desk in front of me. I can't even do the math work. Ratios, coordinates, planes. I ask myself "why do we spend so much time on this crap?" I was even in calculus in high school. Trigonometry! I would have been better off to have learned how to drain a garbage disposal and learn plumbing or harvest a field to learn about the earth, dirt and bugs! How to drive a tractor! How to permaculture and heal the earth! I look up to the class that sits in silence, glued to their screens. Each student has a Chrome Book staring at animated characters with bright colors and funny, silly music learning about math.

Are we moving further away from concrete reality?

Yesterday I observed a teacher read to a middle school class a great story about Humpty Dumpty, renewing himself with wings after falling off the wall. There was a bird inside him! I enjoyed that story!

The teacher of Humpty Dumpty had to describe to the students the meaning of the story, as when she had finished the story, all the children shouted that the story was fake, not real. I stood in suspended belief, as the students, naysayers every single one of them, was unable to understand that a story is something bigger than real or not. . . it's in between where our hearts and our imaginations drive our existence, our future and who we are as people. What has happened to our imaginations!

I think of all the princesses . . . Cinderella and Snow White. Isn't it about time to renew their stories and how they divorce their husbands who turned out to be abusers as they become Queens and heal our lands! Okay, maybe we need our brothers, but let's remember which guys stick by us when we get old.

There's another book at the teacher's desk and I find a quote. "Beneath every behavior is a feeling. And beneath every feeling is a need when we meet that need rather than focus on the behavior. We being to solve the cause and not the symptom." Ashley Warner - Psychologist.

February 2020, Marin County

I had to borrow $40 from my daughter which surely demonstrates the lowest of the low I have ever been in my life time. Borrowing gas money from my 17 year old daughter! I'm literally flat broke. A full tank of gas is a third of my day's pay. My insurance is due in two weeks, which is equal to three days pay. My rent is equal to two weeks of my pay, though I don't get paid for holiday or breaks, so that will factor in differently. I have college debt which is equal to about three days of work and I have credit card debt which is almost a week's worth of work.

Just fifteen years ago I used to make $90 an hour at a corporation selling sofas from a catalog. Now I am in charge of the mental health, physical health and academic health of thirty kids at a time, on some days, and my day rate is almost equal to an hourly rate that I made fifteen years ago, with benefits, mind you.

The system is upside down and backwards.

My daughter said to me, "Mom, you have a Master's degree and you're a teacher. I work at an ice cream store and I'm 17 years old. You have to borrow money from me?"

She's disgusted. I am too. Rent is due in two days and I have nothing. How will I get past this one?

I look around at the wealth in this county of Marin. How many drive in $80K cars and live in palaces. The car they drive their child in to school is equal to my rent for four years. And here I am doing their slave work ensuring their schools look good to ensure property value stays healthy and they maintain their assets?

What has happened to the workers?

I think about the immigrants in this community. They work as nannies, housekeepers, gardeners and roofers. They make pitiful wages but the community can share a narrative that they are "helping" these immigrants because they got it much better here than they did in their home countries.

The immigrants, mostly, are illegal and won't fight for economic equity in fear of their safety as well as their livelihood. After all, it's better here than where they came from. But that is not helping our society. I do agree with Trump on what statement - no one should run from their country. No one should feel that need. So, what happened, is we have taken on the burden of their fear and they get abused here too, bringing down collectively the workers' networth. We need to address this - while protecting people, too. But, then again, who is protecting me? And why do others believe I have to be their protectors?

As a teacher managing up to 40 kids per day, my pay is about $2/hour more than my 17 year old high school daughter serving ice cream.

This is why my father chose to risk everything in 1981. This is why a union stood up to a president to demand honesty and fair contracts. And as we lost everything in that strike, growing up broke and angry, I recognize now that having little money isn't the problem. It's whether or not you have guts that matter in this big world of ours.

It's time to have guts, peacefully. Always with peace.

February 2020, Marin County

I overheard a conversation in the staff lunch room.

"I can't believe a sub cancelled last minute. A sub! How fucked up is that?

Another teacher chimes in. "Well, I heard a tree crashed into her home during the storm last night."

The teacher doesn't reply. Not even with a regret for his thoughts. It's called sub bashing. I see it often, especially when kids misbehave and you mention it to the office. Everyone sanctions it! Be rude and unruly to the substitute teachers! Like it's a cultural habit to be proud of in our society!

I heard it again during the start of another class where a teacher met me early in the morning to go over the material. I asked her why she was there, as often teachers will just leave notes given they are usually at home sick.

"Oh, we have so many problems with no show subs."

I wondered why , but then I knew why. Bad pay, horrific treatment, no benefits.

An electric Trek bike ridden by a middle schooler passes by as I walk to my car. The cost of his bike is worth about the same as my monthly rent.

"You don't belong to a union?" I asked the Transitional kindergarten teacher. I liked her a lot. A strong Latin woman who does not take bullshit, but delivers a tremendous amount of love and good healthy structured play for the children. She's a master.

"They kicked us out because we aren't credentialed teachers."

I sit in the classroom with her. The children are provided breakfast and we sit like civilized people, practice the rest of the world could use. The children are incredibly confident and caring. The food is almost inedible. I look at the teacher and she puts her finger to her lips, to remain silent and not to complain. The kids have learned too to leave the inedible food alone and everyone understands this game without talking about it. All the food is wrapped in plastic. Milk from a cow without choices and I can I assure you the vegan impulse in me wants to scream.

I look at the teacher. Again she doesn't use words, but I know what she is saying. "Keep your mouth quite."

I unfortunately have a real hard time doing that.

March 2020, San Francisco

I had one class left today. I never know what to expect when I walk into a classroom. I've slowly developed a nose for the energy. If children are angry, mentally vacant, respectful or just weird. Yes, kids can be weird and I dare say it's their right and we adults crush that weirdness out of them at too early an age.

I got into the classroom early. Nice light came through the windows and I looked for the sub notes. The kids were reading a book about gangs. Apparently it was a popular book. My instructions were to have the kids read the book out loud.

Another teacher came in. He would be the assistant. He had a strong gait to him, like he played sports and he was intent on making a touchdown with that monomaniacal sense about him. He made it very clear that this was a rough bunch and don't take anything personal. I got ready. It takes a mental exercise and physical one too where you breathe in the concept that it's just 90 minutes of your life, give it your all, be patient, keep your smile, don't get angry, stay centered and don't let them get you. Then that energy needs to go all the way through your body so you can stay grounded. I don't know how else to explain it.

A few boys walked in. They are really young men, and beautiful young men. But, I saw the anger and immediate "fuck you" attitude towards me. But, I turned on the kindness. One sat at his table, legs extended in the fashion statement that "I don't give a fuck about anything." He would be a trouble maker, but what is a trouble maker? A person who has experienced trauma and is trying to figure out his place in the world when so many others have told him that he's a trouble maker?" I wonder.

Other boys walked in, either Hispanic or Black. They didn't want to be there.

The other teacher walked in. He talked tough to the boys about their manners and behavior and then he left. I thanked him and then asked the boys to pull out their books to read. They did reluctantly except for one who had walked over to the window and just stared out. I decided to leave him alone for the moment and focus on the other seven kids, all boys in the class.

"Who would like to read?" I ask.

Of course, no one wanted to read and so they didn't even answer me. I took a good glance around the room. I could feel the trauma they live with. Maybe with family, neighborhood, school, teachers? Who knew and figured there was only one thing I could really do and that was to bring a force calm and nurturing into this time together. So, that's what I did.

I began to read using a soft voice. I walked around the classroom gently as I read and something began to happen. I could see their bodies begin to relax. No one spoke out with interruptions. The energy began to shift. I kept reading.

The boy by the window sat down in a bing bag chair near the window and pulled out what I thought was his phone device, staring at it. But the others kept their calm and I kept reading calmly with a smile in my heart. And when I came to violent passages, I read like I cared about the characters and their own hearts, making comments like "ah, that poor guy" and offering side notes that life can be tough but we also can learn to become kinder.

I finished the chapter and asked the others to finish reading quietly. Now it was time to talk to the young Hispanic boy by the window. I approached him gently and squatted down.

"Would you like to come join us now and finish reading our book."

"I am reading." he said.

"Oh, what are you reading?"

"Gulliver's Travels."

Gulliver's Travels? A book of high literature, one that encapsulates the freedom of travel, discovery and human spirit, one of my favorite books of all time and that I read in college! And here was a teen boy I thought was a trouble maker when in fact he just didn't want to read a book about modern day violence, a book the teacher likely picked thinking the students would engage because it was familiar ground? Maybe. I've seen teachers do that, instead of offering books of inspiration and imagination.

"Gulliver's Travels?" I answered him and smiled. "It's a beautiful book."

The Aftershock of Neoliberal Education

Not only is it a beautiful book, it is one of the most powerful collective stories demonstrating the journey of learning about diversity, power, corruption, greed and more through a nonfiction, beautifully written narrative that takes you to the deepest parts of the imagination.

The other teacher walked back into the classroom hot, like he was ready to bounce on someone acting out. But, instead I think he was shocked by what he saw, that the students were doing something that they normally don't do.

I point to the young Latino kid who looked like he's doing nothing in the corner of the room, near the open windows where the sun is shining. "He's reading Gulliver's Travel, one of the most important books of literature. Did you know that?" I said to the young teacher.

I'm not sure the teacher knew the book! He just gave me a blank look with no response. And then suddenly he didn't know what to do.

Our children are beautiful. And we have to believe that.

Transitional K Class, Marin County

I get to play today. And I'm always educated by how different teachers in this journey of mine administer lessons of art, stories and more. As high tech videos, loud obnoxious songs and dances get projected boldly onto the front screen for the children to mimic, the lost art of quiet nurturing, sweetness and gentle children's play has been slowly disappearing. And we wonder why our children are so wild.

It's art time in this transitional K class, a class that has always perplexed me. A new label of many labels fighting to be recognizes to give someone credit for being the "founder" of a new movement. I used to think the Chinese grandmothers had the sharpest elbows in China, those who knew how to muscle their way around train stations and bus lines. But, I've grown to believe it's Americans who are out to make a name for themselves. So, now it's Transitional Kindergarten and not Pre K and we all have to submit. Can we just keep it simple? Please?

It's art time. We have loads of playdough and finger painting. The kids are mostly again from Latin American origins. I hear some beautiful Spanish being spoken and the children play nicely.

I enjoy the little ones, when you can think the most important lessons in these early years is how to get along with one another. How to be a good friend. How to be nice and kind. How to share.

As I think about it, most adults in our society must have flunked this class. Maybe we should start again.

Now, it's time to read a story. The teacher picked out the book for me. Sometimes I'm able to choose, those who understand having flexibility and choice allows a teacher to do his or her best.

But not today. I must read *The Life of George Washington* to a class of twenty kids from Central America, all of whom spoke Spanish as a first language. Most Guatemalan where Tikun Uman, the last Mayan warrior, stood up against the Spanish and said that he would rise again one day.

This book was NOT my choice, but I read it dutifully, about a white man, a general, who was brave, came from hardship and took on the beginning empire where we live today. The kids listened carefully but I was so horrifically horrified to read this story to these children. There was nothing about his slaves or mass murder of indigenous people, likely for obvious reasons, given their age. But here I am, as a white woman, uplifting a man of violence and initiated the first wave of colonialism, glorifying Washington as our first president.

Now, with all fairness, perhaps we can acknowledge that war gets us nowhere. Washington has carried the narrative of protecting the oppressed people of England who left looking for freedom after being abused. But when does it stop? When do the oppressed become the oppressors? It's an ongoing cycle that must stop.

After I do my duty of reading the story, and watching the children with big eyes watch me word for word tell a lie about history, believing and trusting me, I put the book down and looked straight at these beautiful children.

"Okay, kids, do you think the president is powerful?"
"YES!", they answered.
"Okay, tell me in our country who is MORE powerful?"
"Angels!" One cried out.
"Well, that's possible, but who is alive with skin and bones and is more powerful?"
"Jesus!"
"Okay, well, we're getting maybe closer, at least he had flesh and bones. Who else would be more powerful who is alive TODAY?"
"God!"
"Okay, this is the deal. Someone like you and me and has blood running through their body and breathes oxygen?"
Dead silence.

"YOU!" I say. "Me!" I say.
I've stumped them.
They look at me dumfounded with cocked heads.
"We, the people" are the most powerful force in our country. Don't you forget it, kiddoes!"

It may take a few years for them to revolutionize, but I am planting the seeds.

This idea is not mine. In fact, the idea that teaching youth to challenge authority was a major part of the early education models of Reggio Emelio founder Loris Malaguzzi, born in Italy in 1920. His life confronted fascism, an experience for him that imparted great wisdom to his approach to teaching. He had expressed that people who "conformed and obeyed were dangerous," and it was important to nurture children to maintain their own visions and "think and act for themselves" according Peter Moss, UCL Institute of Education University College London. Malauzzi aligns early education to political practice, as a path toward a democratic, free thinking society, a profound concept.

It's time now to take the kids to a bona fide art class, with a bona fide, certified, credentialed and educated early childhood art teacher. I walk them from the classroom down the hall and put them into a new classroom onto a carpet with a teacher sitting high.

Today's pre K classes require four year olds to sit on the carpet squished together without touching, hitting, pinching or crying for fifteen minutes while they listen to a history lesson of Aboriginal art from a place far away called Australia. I look out my window to the mountains of Marin County and wonder why we can't just make roly poly snakes out of play dough like I did in kindergarten. Better yet, can't we find a mud puddle and let them at it? Mud cakes were the delight in my youth. Those were the best days. Today, you've got kids getting upset if they have messy sand on their hands for two minutes too long. I'm not joking about that either. A topic for another time about the level of toxic uber hygiene our kids are now projecting!

The fancy schmancy art teacher sat the children at the tables with perfectly placed paper, paintbrush and paints. I was honestly impressed. The kids weren't because those perfectly placed paper, paintbrushes and paints were immediately placed in a chaotic pattern to satisfy the children's tastes.

With a few "excuse me, stop hitting, look at me, silence please" the teacher finally shared "You must do as I do with q tips, no swishing color, no painting. . . ONLY DOTS."

Do you have any idea of the amount of "Nos" you end up telling the kids? Do you have any idea of how much information they will never remember or even care about when you feed them information about a far away people and dictate to them how to make the most annoying dots to mimic a far away art in order to make it look so perfect that parents and administrators will be in awe of your teaching?

Who the hell cares if it's a dot or a streak! Who cares at this age!

Bring in the mud! Better yet, send the kids outside to play with the mud!

The only ones who care are the adults who get to brag their four year old kids are learning high level art, while their kids are being shut down of their natural creative talents. They are learning authoritarianism . . . and how to be a puppet for praise. That is my true analysis of pre k and k education (and beyond today) without a purposeful, practical practice of grace and manners that's integrated into a culture of learning. In my book, it's called academic abuse and knocking down free thinking and free creation. Period. Hands down.

Friday, March 13 - Marin County

Some would call this day an ominous day. Others would call this the day the women rise and stand up to the patriarchy which has ruined the value of the matriarchy. Still many may call it the beginning of fascism or big pharma/big tech coup. All I know is it's my last day of work, the last day of school. We all know it even if there hasn't been a formal announcement. Schools are closing across the county, across the world. It's a virus that has taken hold of us, therefore, as a substitute, there will be no pay, not sick leave, no insurance, no letters of love from students. Nothing.

But I choose to give the students something.

I have carte blanch today. As we begin to learn that the schools are closing on Monday and we all carry this feeling of uncertainty, the teacher tells me to do what I would like, given what she had planned makes no sense since the kids won't be in class the following week. Little did we know, it'd take a year.

I proposed an offering.

The school has a rich black community. I had asked the student in the first period if they had ever heard of Harry Belafonte. One white kid in the class knew the son "Day-O". It was a start.

So I chose, on this day, to share a film with the students. It would be my last hurrah, my opportunity to feed a sense of hope, perhaps seed an opportunity into someone who will one day strike a lead and take down the insanity that I have witnessed these months in public schools and society.

I play the film "Sing Your Song," he documentary of the life of Harry Belafonte.

The first five minutes are rioting and speak to our times today facing off racism, inequities and economic challenges, much like Belafonte addressed during the days of Martin Luther King, Jr.

"There is a lot of people who are really pissed off. We are angry, upset. We look around for comfort, but don't find any. Well, we have to look to ourselves. The last frontier of truth is the people themselves!"

The room falls quiet. The youth are captivated, stunned by the power of the narrative. Emboldened by the fact that none of them had ever heard of Belafonte, one of the leading social justice activists who is still alive! How is it possible too many have forgotten? It's been forgotten because our education these last forty years made it disappear. And the youth today should be outraged.

It's going to be a long lesson when this class ends, a determination of how well we have all studied and learned. How do we end the lesson? The lesson about humanity.

I take one look around at these beautiful children and think of all the beautiful children and good teachers I have been graced to meet this past year, knowing our lives are about to take a heavy turn. And I wish for the world to hear the words of Harry Belafonte during this turn. Will it be a direction for the better good or will we dive into a deeper and darker lesson?

My tear drop in the darkness as the film flickers in the classroom. As a global society we have endured all the lessons possible about how to co exist. We have the history books of wars and genocide, The Renaissance, arts, cultures and over 2000 years of history that we have all endured. Every society has had its story of trauma or created trauma. History has been our schooling and as we walk out of the classroom and into the streets of society today, we must ask ourselves whether we have truly learned how to be decent human beings, how to work together and how to share our dreams.

The bell rings and the students pile out. I clean up the teacher's desk. I close the windows and draw the curtains. I take one last glance of the classroom recognizing I have been the student this past year, learning my power as a human being, as a teacher. As I close the door and lock it, I enter a new classroom, the real classroom of life as a new textbook narrative begins.

April, 2020

It's been one month now and this Corona Virus has upset the entire world. We don't know yet, but we, the people are political pawns in what is the most contested political election in the history of the world, that we know. Bernie Sanders has suspended his campaign and that hope for us working poor have had our hopes squashed due to this other virus of pure greed that been driving our country, our schools and our entire lives.

I received the last of my paychecks which amounted to about $800. My rent is $1550 which is nonnegotiable, though my State of California has issued a moratorium on evictions. But that does not take away the fact I'll merely be in debt paying for rent when I have no income. I've managed to get my credit card bills deferred, but not the interest. So I'll end up paying more on my credit cards. My college debt is deferred until August but I have other bills to pay, including Comcast in order to feed a billionaire CEO, as well as PG&E bill and wondering if our community will burn down due to its negligence this next fire season. I wonder. Trump is calling for the shut down of another major public service - the United States Postal Service. My grandfather, who was once a mail carrier and proud WW2 Veteran is rolling in his grave right now.

Bernie suspended his campaign with still many states needing to vote. He got cornered into endorsing Biden. And I just can't go there. Not right now anyway.

I've applied for food stamps, unemployment insurance and started a garden using seeds from the different fruits in my fridge. Last week I walked the neighborhood collecting dandelion seeds to plant. I heard once that a Spanish community survived a war by cultivating dandelions.

My daughter's school has offered food to all the students. So, I road my bike there this morning to pick up those supplies. In the bag included Cocoa Puffs, Fruit Loops, Dorritos, Pop Tarts, a hamburger, french fries, fish sticks and chocolate milk, along with some cranberries, raisins and one fresh orange. Are they trying to make us diseased too?

Trump just launched a new military arm - Space Force and 5G got launched along with Elon Musk's Starlink, with no public outcry.

The silence against these injustices are symbolized by the masks covering mouths that are now ubiquitous in the streets today. I think of Paul Simon's song "The Sounds of Silence." How right that song is.

I purchased a Burka to prove a point publicly, to hopefully jar those around me, in that this is the direction we are all headed. There is talk about chipping people. Not only has our education gone from bad to worse wit online schooling, but our civil rights are disappearing one by one.

Discussions of immunity give rise too. And I look at this packaged food from the local school, one of the most elite school districts in our country, and it makes me physically ill. Corporations dominate our food industry, while they poison our children. The virus isn't just Corona.

We have become the products of the virus of greed, exploitation and fear.

President Jimmy Carter once gave a speech, the Crisis of Confidence. Perhaps it's time to begin our teaching. . . and maybe some of his preaching, finally, after 40 years of darkness, perhaps light will begin to reveal itself in the spirit of Starr King, who represented the spirit of unity.

2021 - Full Circle

October, 2021, Marin County

I have been offered a job at a local public school! It feels like such a fit and I know I can do the job well. The pay will sustain me with another afternoon job at a private school and I can finally be on my way to paying off my bills. I breathe. I can finally breathe. My hard work is paying off.

I'm still subbing now that schools are open. One teacher always called me but one day she told me my name wasn't on the sub list anymore. I figured there was a technical error. I covered her anyway and we did the paper work as needed so I could get paid for the day. The school even upped the pay for subs to $200 a day, a reasonable pay that could actually help me!

Meanwhile I took the time to fill out all the paperwork, get another FBI check for $60 and complete other requirements for the offered job. I dropped off the paperwork to the district office.

And then it all came undone. Just like that. They denied me the work and would not accept a religious exemption for the Covid vaccine. They wouldn't even accept me being tested once a week like other schools have done. They just cancelled me. Gone. Zilch. Nada.

The Aftershock of Neoliberal Education

I had been terminated by Marin County schools too without even so much as being notified with a phone call, a text message or an email. I just disappeared from their system.

I don't know quite how to describe the feeling. There are no words for it. Giving your heart and then getting dumped. I've been down a similar road, in my former marriage, and I know crying about it doesn't help. Now, how am I going to financially survive without ending up in the streets?

I called my dad.

"You know dad, you taught me something in 1981 when you stood up to the government with your terms for fair wages and honesty in politics and lost your job for it," I said.

He listened.

"Well, I just stood up myself and lost my job. And I'm still standing."

And in my heart I hoped it wouldn't take another 40 years for the truths to shine, as they are now about President Ronald Reagan's myth and the brilliance of President Jimmy Carter's administration. Have we learned yet?

Is it time to remove the mask? And I don't refer to the one forced on us these last two years. I refer to the mask of the last 40 years. It's time to show who we have been and why. It is time to start talking about the last 40 years and end The Reagan Era as we begin to revolutionize a new era of collaboration, cooperation, education, humility, kindness, respect and peace.

As Carter said in the Crisis of Confidence Speech, it can be the greatest exploration ever. And as Belafonte said "We have to look to ourselves. The last frontier of truth is the people themselves!"

We have learned our lessons.

Yes, we have.

Afterwards

Sitting in the mineral bath in my old, out of shape, and too tight bikini, I feel the bubbles around me, like little champagne bursts. Oak trees dangle around and above with sweeping Old Man's Beard. I fall into revere thinking about President Teddy Roosevelt. When did I ever think about him in my life?

You know the guy, right? Okay, I admit it. I knew zilch about him two days ago myself other than I knew he had been a president, which was, of course a dead giveaway due to the title. And I learned something else. He sat in this very hot tub where I am trying to collect my soul and perhaps absorb some truth and collective soul making for my world. I am at the mineral springs of Vynchi Hot Springs here in Northern California, a historic marvel that not only mixes a Native American narrative of healing waters but also of a Northern California history that nearly escaped with the wind.

I listen to the wind. It's always worked for me. It's like I can hear the voices of time lingering and wafting. Here I am at a historic land that is out of my budget (thank you US Bank for the credit card loan), a lodge I'm visiting with my daughter, a full moon night retreat to escape so much insanity that is driving our world.

So, in this moment I choose to listen to the dead voices around me. The wind. It's comforting.

Indeed, Mark Twain used to talk to me, too. He even played tricks on me. Tricks. Just because he's dead, don't believe for a second that he's dead. His spirit is very much alive, when you attune to dead spirits. They have left messages for us. Antidotes, truths, wisdom, inspiration and spirit. I few years ago I found a stone statue of Mark Twain in South Lake Tahoe, just sitting on a bench looking at the far away mountains. I sat with him in the quiet as the snow was falling around us. But it wasn't so quiet. I could hear Mark Twain screaming at us with one of his favorite adages – "Education consists mainly of what we have unlearned."

Brett Harte who was a Twain's buddy until they had a falling out was almost screaming at me recently when I discovered his writing about the slaughtering of the Wiyots Indigenous community just right north of me now, a bit of inconvenient history that has gotten missed these last one hundred years, at least in my education. Where is the acknowledgement that he risked his life to share a brutal story of children, women and men being killed in these parts. near my bubble champagne mineral bath? After Harte, the journalist, wrote the story of the slaughter, he ran for his life due to death threats about his own life!

At this same time, Twain had kept pushing his books and wit on me. I see him everywhere. The draw was so strong a summer or two ago, that I loaded my kids into the car to visit Twain Harte. It's a town in the mountains. Me and the kids walked the town with its old time wood planked shops filled with bookstores and cafes and tourist trinkets. I could feel him luring me to something as I sat next to a tree. I know it sounds crazy, but it's not crazy once you can listen to these subtleties. That night I got online to find something that spoke to me. And I found his book, one that wasn't even published until years after his death, a manuscript that he had dedicated to his wife. And it was profoundly teasingly surreal when I looked down on the curb one day and there it was - a book calling for me. Aside from the American classics of *Huckleberry Finn*, *Tom Sawyer*, *The Prince and The Pauper* and *Joan of Arc*, was a very unknown book call *Letters from Earth*, a collection of essays that were written during a difficult time in Twain's life; he was deep in debt and had lost his wife and one of his daughters.

He wrote as if he was a dejected angel on earth with a sharp criticism about religions.

I think of all this as I sink deeper into the earthly minerals, sacred water where the Wiyots would come to bathe. I listen to the wind. There is comfort here.

How is it possible I knew nothing about these mineral baths two weeks ago? As a native northern Californian, I have missed out on our local natural wonders, places where I can connect to our history, our LIVING history?

Just a few weeks ago I scavenged for mushrooms in the forest, learning about these incredible fruits of mycelium that rage under foot, with mysteries. Porcini, chanterelles, hedgehogs, candy caps. How is it possible I never learned about these natural wonders in school but I learned buzz words for technology, corporate logos and commercialization to feed a system that has exploited me for profit?

It was just late spring I followed a 10,000 year ritual, discovering another part of my home state - The Lost Coast. I joined herbalists and spiritualists to harvest seaweed from the shores, an act women, or mostly women, would journey along the shores each year to harvest, dry and preserve to feed their communities, connecting with the ocean and celebrating that which is natural. We even made a spa-like cream with seaweed and oatmeal, lathering it onto our bodies and laid near the river like sirens of another age. A water snake slithered on the glassy water surface to visit us. And all along I kept understanding how far removed I've been from where I live, even though I've been right here. I've missed out on the historic and often lost stories of mountains, people and plants because I've been journeying far from home, listening to an education that took me far from who I am and where I am.

As I set out for my next adventure, I plan to honor what my great uncle once said to me when he saw me getting prepped for a journey to China. "Why do you want to go all the way there when you have everything right here?"

As I live next to a great mountain, Mount Tamalpais, my next journey will be to connect with it, feel it and explore it, a place that is known as the Sleeping Lady. The mountain will be my healing center, after all that we have endured these last few years, these last 40 years and these last 2000 years. We are our ancestors. We are from our ancestors. And something tells me they are whispering to us all to learn from them, their history, so we can be better people today.

I will learn to eat from the great oaks and laurel trees, acorns to bay nuts, food that was part of my ancient Celtic heritage too, a remembrance of my ancestors who faced *Per Ardua* or "through adversity," an idea to get through hard times and make the most of it with celebration and honor and wit, that which does not cost a cent nor gives a cent to another's power. I will learn every trail and walk barefoot to feel the essence of what we have instead of those who turned their back on what is natural in this tech dominated, exploitative era. And I will one day introduce myself, as the Maori have shared with us, as a way of honor:

My name is Barbara McVeigh. I am of Mount Tamalpais in a land called Marin named after a great Miwok Chief and near a City called San Francisco named after a saint where the ocean meets a great bay. My ancestors are the Celts, a history nearly deleted, but we are still here.

It's time for all of us to come home and remember who and what we are. To see where we are and where we come from. A time to honor ancestors and the children of the future. Can we call it humility? Or, is it courage?

It's time for a new era.

www.ingramcontent.com/pod-product-compliance
Lightning Source LLC
LaVergne TN
LVHW051555070426
835507LV00021B/2594